SEPT 2016

SWIMMING UPSTREAM

TO JULIET

CONTINUE TO INSPIRE!

ENDORSEMENTS

"To say that I was completely captivated by your story is an understatement. It is compelling, authentic, uplifting and very insightful. The experiences and challenges you describe so vividly, being a female in executive management and inside the boardroom, strongly resonated for me. *Swimming Upstream* is written from the heart and with intelligence. It is a must read for everyone and in particular for women in business or at the start of their career, who will find inspiration, encouragement, excellent guidance and strength in the story and the lessons learned."

Aletha Ling, Senior Vice President Operations, Emerging Markets Digital, Visa Cape Town

"A testimony to the indomitable human female spirit. A must read for all African women."

Richard Barrett, author, speaker and Chairman of the Barrett Values Centre

"One of the most impressive autobiographies in recent years under the catchy title, *Swimming Upstream*, a riveting account of how a young black woman, called Shirley Zinn, rises from the stifling conditions of the Cape Flats under apartheid to take a doctorate from Harvard and eventually become one of the leading human resources professionals in the country today. What makes this well-written book particularly relevant in the present is that it draws attention to the role of non-material resources in shaping the destiny of disadvantaged youth in circumstances where there was little money and even fewer opportunities."

Prof Jonathan Jansen, Rector and Vice-Chancellor of the University of the Free State

"A heart-breaking and heart-warming commentary on a life of stress and success. Moving and inspiring and brave."

Joan Joffe, business leader turned 'venture catalyst'

"*Swimming Upstream* is more than just an autobiography, it's a must-have national conversation. What differentiates top leaders like Prof Shirley Zinn from others, and is at the very heart of this excellent read, is a conscious understanding that education and learning are tools used to build a destiny and legacy on a foundation of honourable values and sound moral principles. Where these values are vapid and principles skewed, we find success that is either stunted or blighted by self-serving attitudes and behaviours. Where they are straight and true, we find Shirley and a few other rare individuals.

Shirley's story serves as a guiding light and foundational framework for all future young leaders, and a sounding board and moral compass for established leaders and their teams."

Gareth Armstrong, Executive Director, future CEOs™

"This is the story of a remarkable South African woman. Having reached the top in her field, from the most meagre of beginnings, she shows us what feminism can be and she makes it clear how important diversity is, in any organisation; how the thoughts and solutions of a diverse group surpass those of any group of like-minded folks. A real bonus for a country like South Africa."

Eleanor Duckworth, Professor Emerita, Harvard University

"How strong is your inner core? How would you respond when life throws its toughest challenges at you? Some may wallow in self-pity, some may externalise the cause and seek an external refuge, and then there is the rare breed who are galvanised by the experience. *Swimming Upstream* is the compelling story of Shirley Zinn who took life's pain, who bounced back and who is still rising."

Trevor Manuel, former Minister in the Presidency for the National Planning Commission

"*Swimming Upstream* is a moving and gripping account of the life shifting, life shaping and life shattering events that define its highly successful author, Shirley Zinn. It's extremely rare for a person of her prominence, profile and accomplishment to permit such unfettered, unrestricted, open and candid access to her heart, soul and vulnerabilities.

A compelling and captivating read, this book is the infectious story of the author's immense tenacity, unshakeable resilience and unwavering stubborn will to succeed. It's the story of her courageous, cathartic and heroic journey through life. It's her story of overcoming the extremely arduous and seemingly unfair challenges life has thrown her way. It's her story about swimming upstream and, despite the scars, finding a way to survive."

Richard Pike, Chief Executive Officer, Adcorp Holdings Limited

"Every now and then a generation casts to the fore a personality who stands firmly as a luminous lamp pole and fountain of inspiration. Shirley Zinn, accomplished academic and unwavering intellect, exemplary and inspirational corporate leader particularly in the crucial field of human resources, is a worthy representative of our generation and what it bequeaths to posterity. I commend and recommend her autobiography as enlightening reading."

Prof Reuel Khoza, former Chairman of Nedbank

"Shirley Zinn is an extraordinary individual. Her personal journey is one of remarkable resilience, courage, and inspiration. Her extraordinary educational achievements are a result of her hard work and her continual pursuit of excellence. Her impressive professional career is a record of her outstanding contributions and impact. *Swimming Upstream* is a must-read for anyone who wants a life of meaning and purpose."

Esther Benjamin, CEO, Africa Operations, Laureate International Universities and Monash South Africa

"Professor Shirley Zinn's life and career story is one of triumph over adversity and loss. It will pull every string in your heart and inspire at the same time. *Swimming Upstream* is a page turner that offers hope for every South African while providing powerful lessons on being an authentic leader in today's complex world."

Professor Stella M Nkomo, University of Pretoria

"In her well-written autobiography, *Swimming Upstream*, Shirley Zinn shares the extraordinary story of her life, where she honestly reflects upon her past and the ways in which she conquered the hardships that she encountered along her journey. Shirley's passion for sport, education and her dedication to discipline gives readers a personal outlook at the unfolding of her life, whereby she delivers an empowering message of hope. Advocating the indispensable qualities of resilience and determination to overrule circumstance, she inspires the reader to delve into their innermost depths in order to triumph in the face of adversity. Shirley is also an advocate for a cause that is inextricably close to my heart and that is a dire need for men and women to unite over: eradicating the invisible presence of the 'glass ceiling' in order to achieve the transcendence of gender parity on every front.

Having profoundly resonated with Shirley's sentiments regarding the life lessons that are obtained through sport as well as with her tireless devotion to discipline and excellence, it is evident that the message conveyed in *Swimming Upstream* is universally meaningful and applicable to a diverse audience.

Shirley clearly demonstrates the liberating realisation that a conscious desire to succeed significantly outweighs the dictates of one's circumstances at birth. I recommend this book to anyone seeking a glittering dose of empowerment, mentorship and above all, inspiration."

Jenna Clifford – Founder & Director of Jenna Clifford Design Jewellers, Torchbearer to the United Nations Millennium Development Goals 3 Campaign for Gender Equality and Women Empowerment

"The courage, compassion and resilience that took Shirley on her journey from the Cape Flats to corporate leadership were all attributes needed for the part she played in transforming Nedbank into a vision led and valued driven company."

Tom Boardman, former Nedbank CEO

"This autobiographical account embodies the very spirit of success, achieved sometimes, against all odds.

South Africa needs inspirational role models like Shirley Zinn whose vision for this country and understanding of leadership are a blueprint for survival, tenacity, strength and reaching the top while retaining one's humanity. It is a must-read for us all.

Karla Fletcher, Director, Topco Media

SWIMMING UPSTREAM

A story of grit and determination to succeed

by

Shirley Zinn

2016

Copyright © KR Publishing and Shirley Zinn

All reasonable steps have been taken to ensure that the contents of this book do not, directly or indirectly, infringe any existing copyright of any third person and, further, that all quotations or extracts taken from any other publication or work have been appropriately acknowledged and referenced. The publisher, editors and printers take no responsibility for any copyright infringement committed by an author of this work.

Copyright subsists in this work. No part of this work may be reproduced in any form or by any means without the written consent of the publisher or the author.

While the publisher, editors and printers have taken all reasonable steps to ensure the accuracy of the contents of this work, they take no responsibility for any loss or damage suffered by any person as a result of that person relying on the information contained in this work.

First published in 2016

ISBN: 978-1-86922-589-6
eISBN: 978-1-86922-590-2 (PDF eBook)

Published by KR Publishing
P O Box 3954
Randburg
2125
Republic of South Africa

Tel: (011) 706-6009
Fax: (011) 706-1127
E-mail: orders@knowres.co.za
Website: www.kr.co.za

Printed and bound: Creda, Eliot Avenue, Epping II, Cape Town, 7460, www.creda.co.za
Typesetting, layout and design: Cia Joubert, cia@knowres.co.za
Cover design: Cia Joubert, cia@knowres.co.za
Cover photograph: Photographic Studio, info@aphotographicaffair.co.za
Editing and proofreading: Mandy Collins, mcollins@icon.co.za
Project management: Cia Joubert, cia@knowres.co.za

Dedication

This book is dedicated to my son, Jamie.

FOREWORD

Swimming Upstream, **a story of grit and determination,** is perhaps our post-apartheid affliction: everyone has a story to tell. There is no shortage of books on the market about heroic individuals from both sides of the struggle, such as those who boast without conscience of their feats fighting for the white South African Defence Force and the many black victims (and some white) who recount in bitter detail the horrors of their lives under apartheid. There are books about apartheid spies who feel the need to set the record straight, and others who lament in book-length about having been sold out by an erstwhile comrade. And then there are books that try to rehabilitate an anti-apartheid bomber or re-tell the story of an apartheid big man.

Most times the prose is weak, the storylines cluttered and the social insights slim. But a book there must be. And then along comes one of the most stunning autobiographies in years, *Swimming Upstream*, the account of the life of a child of the Cape Flats who took a doctorate from Harvard and became one of the most powerful women in corporate South Africa. This is the story of Shirley Zinn.

Since I had about half a dozen "forewords" to new books waiting to be written, I decided to open the incoming file, read only the first few lines out of sheer curiosity, with the plan to place this latest manuscript at the back end of the pile of promises to wait its turn. That never happened. From the opening paragraph to the last I was hooked and finished the book in one sitting, after which I reclined in my chair with the satisfied smile of a youngster from Retreat who had just finished a many-layered trifle pudding familiar to those parts of the Cape Flats.

What is it that makes *Swimming Upstream* such a gripping life story? To begin with, it is exceptionally well written, which means that you cannot wait to turn the page. It introduces you to a troubling, dramatic moment but then leaves you hanging for much of the book as you sweat—so what really happened on the national road (N2) as you and your family left Cape Town? Few authors have mastered the skill of writing in ways that engage your emotions, intellect, curiosity and devotion in one sweep and from the first pages. As I furiously dug into the trifle pudding the little bits of jelly and custard and cake went spilling everywhere as I tried to get to the bottom of things, so to speak.

The book is not only well-composed, it unintentionally takes on one of those big social science questions many of us grapple with. Why do some children of disadvantage make such spectacular leaps across the barriers of race, class and, in this case, gender, to such distinction in life? Children in the same families, burdened by hardship and surrounded by poverty, often go in completely different directions – some remain stuck in their misery, others survive in reasonable jobs and a few achieve extraordinary success. Why?

The basic contours of Shirley Zinn's life as a black South African woman are familiar – the stories about forced removals, racial discrimination, unequal education, financial hardship, and the struggle to find work. But there is another layer to the trifle of her remarkable life – of caring family, close friends, community networks, inspiring teachers and parents of faith. Even in the most dire of circumstances there are non-material resources (emotional, spiritual, educational and communal) that can be drawn on and back up an individual's resilience to not be broken by the daily grind of oppression. Throughout her life, Shirley is tempted to give up – find a job, drop studies and simply survive – but she persists against unbelievable odds and comes out not surviving but thriving as arguably our top human resources expert in South Africa today.

The environment is familiar to me – Steenberg and Retreat – and I still wonder how our paths did not at some point cross since we lived one street apart, Shirley's family in 11th and mine in 10th avenue. As I read the manuscript I recognised those dilemmas of Christian faith on the Flats, of embrace as well as exclusion. The hardworking parents who toiled round the clock to make sure every child had a basic education. The fears and uncertainties at every turn as bills struggled to be paid and the campus uprisings drew you in at the same time as they threatened the end of your career dreams. And yet within all of this testing and turmoil there is the one opportunity – to win a bursary or to study overseas. Nobody is more surprised than you when your application is approved. You drop everything, including your job, to get advanced training and then come back to make your difference.

Nothing of course prepares you for studying abroad. You soon find the money is too little and time after time you consider packing up, going home and reuniting with your loved ones. But there is an American friend who sees your need, supports you and embraces your family. You stand up to fight another day for you will never again have such access to brilliant professors and outstanding libraries. Eventually, through all the uncertainty and self-doubt, you make it, and win an Ivy League degree. Some aunts put lemon in a trifle pudding.

You find re-entry is never simple. You are suspect back home and any hint of an accent brings a mix of admiration and alienation. Nobody walks into a job with a top degree from a leading university. And so, for a time, you live in limbo all over again until a small opportunity comes by and this turns into other chances to prove yourself in a country that at the time still put down black professionals as "over-qualified" and where women, especially, would find it difficult to break into the boardrooms of the newly emerging country. Shirley Zinn persists through all of this or, in her compelling metaphor, she swims upstream and finds her way to the top.

The road from the Cape Flats to Harvard to executive leadership in companies like Standard Bank is filled with potholes that can at any time wreck the journey once and for all. But we now know that non-material resources in a disadvantaged community can outweigh the burden of repressive laws and the lack of family finances. We learn that a quality education even in those times of hardship makes an enormous difference when all other routes to success are blocked. And we find that at the end of the day the person matters, when you are driven by a deep desire to go forward in life regardless of the objective evidence facing you—that few in the family or community make it out of the place with the unfortunate name of Retreat.

This book stands out in a crowded field of autobiographies because while it is about Shirley it is also about all of us making that journey then and now. Her story will inspire thousands of young people faced with the same dilemmas about how to proceed when the odds are still stacked against you. Though not intended as a scholarly book, I have no doubt that sociologists of development and community psychologists will find this work a resource to draw on without the clutter of academic verbosity. And for those who are moved by biographies that weave together the personal, the professional and the political in a compelling narrative of an ordinary South African's life, expect a treat of trifle pudding second to none.

Prof Jonathan Jansen
October 2015

PROLOGUE

The December holidays of 2002 were just like all of those that had come before. Every year we did the same thing: we planned a trip to Cape Town, and a camping trip somewhere along the way. Our holidays were all about hiking, braaiing, swimming and walking through the mountains. I was looking forward to the summer break.

Our son, Jamie, loved the outdoors, and he thoroughly enjoyed camping. He would meet old friends and make new ones. We were eager to try out our new caravan, something we'd been planning for years, and we had a new double-cab 4x4 bakkie. We were so grateful and happy for everything we had and had worked so hard for.

My husband, Kevin, also loves the outdoors. It had taken me a bit longer to get used to it, because I like my comforts, but our caravan had a fully loaded bathroom with a loo, so there was no need for me to use the ablution blocks in the campsites.

Jamie was already in Cape Town. Kevin's parents lived with us in Pretoria, and every year they took Jamie with them down to Cape Town. They would fly down together around 10 December, and Jamie would stay with my mom and dad for a week or two, where he was thoroughly spoilt. He would spend time with his cousin, Erin, and have an amazing time.

It had been a year of slog; a very busy year with much travelling abroad. At the time I was the regional head of HR for Reckitt-Benckiser's Africa and Middle East region, and that meant a lot of travel.

Despite it being all work-related, it was still an opportunity for me to explore the world, and I was really enjoying work. At home, I was trying to be the best possible wife and mother. Life was generally happy and it was good. Still, I was really pleased to be on holiday.

Kevin and I drove out of Pretoria on 22 December, and I remember noticing a strange sensation, almost a premonition. I was overly nervous, on edge. And yet I was so looking forward to our ultimate destination, the Berg River Resort in Paarl.

The Christmas traffic was heavy as thousands of people left the province: Gauteng would look like a ghost town by Christmas Day. As we hit the highway people were driving so badly. Truck drivers were heading home with their last loads of cargo and overladen buses sped by at ridiculous speeds. But Kevin, being a very cautious driver, told me to relax and start enjoying the wind-down.

On Christmas Eve we finally arrived at my parents' home in Retreat, Cape Town. There was lots of excitement, and we fell into familiar routines: church, gifts, and taking out the old family Christmas tree with its familiar decorations from my childhood.

Christmas Day was lovely: a wonderful roast lunch with all the trimmings. We were filled with the joy of festivity, family, togetherness, laughs and love – it was perfect.

On Boxing Day, full of the joys of family time together, we headed off to Berg River with our new caravan for a few days. Jamie was proud of it and excited about being able to swim in the river: he was a good swimmer and daring in his outdoor pursuits. If you gave him a diving or swimming challenge, he'd say: "Bring it on!" His two uncles, Andre and Val Steenkamp, also taught him to fish that holiday, and I remember him posing very proudly for a photo with the fish he'd caught.

On our way back we went past Betty's Bay to friends who have a house there. The grandmother of the family had passed away, and there were candles all over the house in her memory. They asked us to stay with them that evening, and the next day we drove back to the southern suburbs of Cape Town for New Year's Eve. We were going to a party and our good friends, Melanie and Melvyn Daniels, were going to babysit Jamie.

On New Year's Night we slept at my mom's place, as my uncle was coming to visit. And on 3 January we would be leaving to return to Pretoria via Mossel Bay. It was a busy time.

But finally, it was time to leave, and we began the packing process. My mom had made crayfish curry, so we tucked into that. The washing machine had been going non-stop. Jamie had about a hundred live garden snails that he'd collected and was carrying around. How he kept them alive for so long nobody knows. And when I told him he couldn't take them in the car like that, he stuffed them all into a giant sized glass jar and pierced the lid a few times for oxygen. Ordinary things on an ordinary family holiday.

We were only going as far as Mossel Bay, so we made a few stops on our way out of Cape Town. We stopped at our friend, Nigel Davids, to wish him for Christmas and New Year, and to give him his gift of a T-shirt. Then we stopped at Sandy, Kevin's sister and Jamie's godmother, and there were hugs and good-byes. And then, finally, we were on the road.

As we drove down Jan Smuts towards the N2 we saw the funeral for the grandmother of our Betty's Bay friends, so we got out at the church to express our sympathies. And then we really were on our way.

Kevin is very precise about how things are done – I think it's his third- or fourth-generation German blood shining through. He always checked that Jamie's seatbelt was on, and he did so as usual. Jamie also knew the rules and that seatbelts were non-negotiable. But as we were driving away from the church, with thoughts of Mossel Bay in our heads, Jamie said to me, "Mom, my seatbelt isn't working." So Kevin said we'd stop at the next garage to sort it out.

We never made it to Mossel Bay. We didn't even make it to the next garage.

Chapter 1

Everyone has a story

Everyone has a story. And our stories are only stories because of others' stories. At birth we're connected to other people's stories – those of our parents and, perhaps, our grandparents and extended families. And some feel the weight of history more acutely than others.

I feel the burden of connectedness with my family's history very heavily: my life is intimately intertwined with the lives of my family members through past and present generations.

I've also realised that my story is inextricably linked to South Africa's history. History is important as it helps us to understand the current landscape and gives us the strength to shape an inspiring future.

Two months after South Africa was declared a republic, independent and outside of the British Commonwealth, I was born at the Somerset Hospital in Cape Town. By that time, my father's family had already left District Six.

My father tells me that his parents had been renting a house in District Six and had to leave for Harfield Village to live in a shack because my grandparents couldn't afford the rent. They later moved to a council house in Steenberg, on the dusty dunes of the Cape Flats, an apartheid dumping ground twenty-five kilometres away, and an area that today is still characterised by very high unemployment, extreme poverty, drugs, gangs, crime, fear, and very little hope.

But before they moved to Steenberg, my father's family lived on the pavement and in makeshift shacks in Harfield Road for many years. The worst part was that the family was split: one child slept here, another slept somewhere else. Life was a continuous struggle. The family foraged for food and shelter on a daily basis.

District Six, a former inner-city residential area in Cape Town, and home to thousands of coloured families, is bounded by Sir Lowry Road in the North, De Waal Drive in the South, Tennant Road to the West and Cambridge Road to the East. The District Six community was destroyed by the apartheid government's programme of forced removals, which started in 1968 and only ended in 1980 when I was nineteen years old.

Forced removals were part of the apartheid regime's attempts to create separate 'group areas' based on race. The Group Areas Act[1], a very complex and key piece of legislation that was at the heart of apartheid's legal framework, was nothing more than deliberate social engineering aimed at segregating people based on the colour of their skin. It was against this backdrop that I was born in Steenberg on 14 July 1961, and my sister, Merle, followed in October 1964.

The Cape Flats are no place to grow up in and a hard place to live in. It's an area that continues to deteriorate to this day. Life in the Cape Flats is tough: gangsters, drugs, alcohol abuse and domestic violence are rife. When I was growing up there, squabbles and fighting were the daily norm. People would literally be killed on your doorstep. There would be running battles through your backyard, over your roof, and through your house. And our house was often in the middle of the gangster-related crossfire.

There were very high levels of poverty: many families lived well below the breadline. There were also very high levels of unemployment, and lots

---

1 The Group Areas Act was the title of three Acts of the Parliament of South Africa enacted under the apartheid government. The Acts assigned racial groups to different residential and business sections in urban areas in a system of urban apartheid. *Source: Wikipedia*

of teenage pregnancies. And there was very little hope for a meaningful future.

Nothing has really changed in the ensuing years. Notorious gangs rule strictly demarcated territories that are no-go zones for other gangs. If you transgress the demarcations, whether you do so purposefully or not, it means war. Gangs are clearly recognisable by their graffiti names on the walls of the sub-economic blocks of flats, and their associated warrior numbers and logo warn you of the area that you're entering.

I've always been inspired by Ralph Waldo Emerson's observation that our past does not define our future: "What lies behind us and what lies before us are small matters compared to what lies within us." But one of the most important lessons that I've learnt in life is that you must never forget who you are, or where you came from. Remain grounded and stay true to your roots.

More importantly, I've also learnt that where you come from doesn't have to influence where you end up in life, but it does require a conscious decision on your part to make something of yourself in spite of your circumstances.

I recall looking at my surroundings and saying to myself at a very young age: "This isn't for me; it's not where I want to be. I want to move out of this situation, and I want to take others with me."

My home, for many years, was a tiny house situated at number 1, 11th Avenue, Steenberg. The house was on a bustling street corner, and there was (and still is) a lot of street noise, as taxis and buses passed our house constantly.

Ours was a council house. Council houses were poorly designed: they were very basic, much like today's RDP houses. However, unlike RDP houses, they were not stand-alone homes: five or six houses were joined together, and people would erect little fences to separate their homes from the neighbours.

Just like all of the other houses, our house only had one bedroom that accommodated a double bed for my parents and a single bed each for Merle and me. The house had a small lounge, a bathroom and a kitchen. There was no bath, hand-basin or shower, and there was only cold running water.

We had to wash in an iron bath. This was quite a lengthy and tedious process, as we had to heat our bath water in a pot over a Primus paraffin stove. We all took turns to bath in that same water. One evening our Primus stove caught alight in the kitchen. It was a terrifying experience and we had to respond very quickly. We threw the primus out the back door and onto the sand to kill the fire.

Because the area has an extremely high water table, winters on the Cape Flats were really cold – the kind of cold that gets into your bones. Heavy rain waters didn't drain away naturally, and with poor formal storm-water systems, rainwater often stood for weeks before it dried up.

Our house, built from low-cost cement blocks and an asbestos roof, was very cold and damp when the winter rains hit. The damp seemed to creep through the concrete slab. Linoleum covered the floors, but this offered no warmth. There was absolutely no means of warming oneself or keeping warm.

As was typical of council houses, there was also very poor insulation, so the house was very draughty. The wind constantly forced its way into the house. You opened the front door and the wind almost blew the door off its hinges, followed closely by merciless driving rain.

People built all sorts of structures to keep the rain out. Even today, people living in council houses still build some sort of alcove above the front door that you can stand under, or rush to without all the wet coming into the house.

But all of that meant that people were often ill with flu, colds or tuberculosis and related chest illnesses. They simply didn't have the immune systems to stand up to those diseases on top of their poor diets and general poverty. Some were so poor that they lived entirely on bread and tea.

When I think of our house in Steenberg, almost forty years later, I can still smell the freshly-painted walls at Christmas time. I also remember the polished floors – good old Cobra polish produced by Reckitt Benckiser for more than a hundred years made the concrete floors shine like glass. It also made the floor very slippery and it was my job to warn the elderly when they visited at Christmas.

While I was writing this book, I decided to drive past our old house and take some photographs. The current owner, Mrs Scheepers, who has lived there for the past thirty-six years, came out to talk to me, and invited Kevin and me in. When I explained who I was and what I intended to do, she was pleasantly overwhelmed.

The house seemed smaller than I remembered. The lounge, the original bedroom, the kitchen and the bathroom remain unchanged, but the outside has since been paved, and two bedrooms have been added. But visiting the house brought back so many memories, and I realised just how much my life has changed for the better. None of my family has ever gone back to the house and no-one else in my family intends doing so. Many memories from this period of our lives are just too painful.

And even now, after all this time, when apartheid has fallen and things have changed so much, it's still a horrendous place for children to grow up – if they grow up at all. Two months after we met Mrs Scheepers, I returned to show her the photos we had taken. But when I arrived, my dad informed me that her eighteen-year-old grandson had been stabbed to death outside her house; a grim reminder of what we were exposed to living there.

This kind of event is very depressing: it's as though time has stood still. Our old neighbours and some of my family still live in the area, and I visit them often. Life has become even more difficult for most. This is the shocking reality of the socio-economic landscape in South Africa

Most are too caught up in trying to survive, and just don't have the energy to fight and swim upstream. It takes tenacity to battle against the tide and overcome the powerful tugs of the undercurrent and the forces so intent on dragging you backwards in life. I was fortunate enough to have parents, grandparents and teachers who gave me the grounding I needed to find my way out.

My dad, James (Jimmy) Jeftha, was born in Cape Town in Van de Leer Street, District Six, on 8 July 1937. He is the third eldest of the nine children (eight boys and one girl) born to Ma and Pa Jeftha, my grandparents. Dad was baptised in St. Mark's Church, Cape Town, and under the provisions of the Group Areas Act they were forced to move to Claremont/Harfield.

In 1943, he first attended St Matthews Primary School and then went on to Rosmead Primary in Standard 4 (Grade 6) and then Livingstone High School. He left school in Standard 7 (Grade 9) and started his first job with Castle Wine at just sixteen.

He met Rosemarie, my mother, at St. Andrew's Church, Steenberg, when he was nineteen, where they practised for variety concerts that were held to raise funds for the church. He gave her the most beautiful necklace for her twenty-first birthday, a treasured possession she still has tucked away safely after all of these years. On June 11, 1960, they were married at St. Cyprians Church, Retreat, and moved into the council house at 11th Avenue. We lived in that house until we moved to Grassy Park in 1974, when I was thirteen.

Both my parents worked up to their retirement, and my mom got my dad a job at Castle Wine in Cape Town where they worked together for many years thereafter. The irony of my dad's career is that he was a teetotaller all his life, which debunks many of the perceptions people have about people living on the Cape Flats being prolific drinkers.

I often joke that this is a great shame since employees at then Castle Wine, and later Distillers, were given samples of the various products that the distillery produced and sold. If Dad had enjoyed a tipple, can you imagine what an interesting cellar he could have built up, having worked for Distillers for forty years?

My dad was a very good sportsman, and introduced us to the rigours of sport at a very young age. He played as a centre for Retreat Rugby Club. He also played cricket for St. Andrews Cricket Club with the rest of the Jeftha brothers. They really gave the other clubs a good run for their money, especially when my grandfather, Pa Jeftha, was the umpire – I understand he never signalled for Leg Before Wicket (LBW) whenever the Jeftha boys batted.

Dad also did weight-lifting, played a serious game of table-tennis and generally kept fit all his life. It's great fun to this day to sit and watch sport with him. Thanks to my dad, I often surprise people with just how much I know about sport. His analysis, predictions and compelling commentating are usually spot-on. While this obsession drives my mother crazy at times (she doesn't share his passion for sport), I'm addicted to sport as a result.

There are some wonderful memories from my childhood that really stand out. I'll never forget the day we got our first car. It was a red Ford Anglia, designed and manufactured by Ford in the UK. Its American-influenced styling was very popular and more than 1.3-million units were sold worldwide.

Bearing in mind that my dad had ridden a bicycle his entire life before this, Merle and I thought it was the greatest thing on earth to finally have a family car of our own. We were so proud of it. Before that, both of us would go places with him on his bicycle. Dad would put Merle on the cross-bar, and I sat on the carrier at the back, which was very hard and uncomfortable. And there was no padding, so I felt every bump in the road.

We went to church and the station like that, on Dad's bike. All shopping was miraculously done every weekend on the bicycle – transporting everything home took some doing. And yet, ironically, I'm a very poor cyclist! But I learnt so much from my father, especially that it was important to have a vision and then work hard towards achieving it.

My dad retired at fifty-six, but he was not someone who could sit around doing nothing. With some encouragement from Kevin and one of his friends, Vincent Murray, my dad set up a table at the Parow flea market on a Saturday. Vincent supplied the electrical goods to sell – extension cords, cables and multi-plugs – which he sold at a small profit.

Dad apparently did the best deals on electrical goods at the market. Everyone would say: "Go to Brother Jimmy." He had his table at the flea market for about a decade and only gave up his stall when the winters became too harsh and the goods too heavy for him to carry.

There was always the principle in our home that you can make something out of nothing. In his ministry, my father always tells people you can make R2 out of R1. You don't have to sit around and allow yourself to flounder economically without doing anything to try to improve your lot.

And he didn't just talk about it – he lived his words. A devout Christian and a lay preacher, he was always very involved in the work of the church in various ways, and still works in the community, visiting the sick and aged at hospital and at home. He even inspires the neighbourhood to take pride in their homes and gardens, which takes some doing.

My dad is a great father, a wonderful grandfather, a great source of inspiration and a real role model to me. He is a man of principle and very high values. Although he never had lots of money to give us, he gave us so much more and for this I am eternally grateful. Instead of giving us the fish, he taught us to fish so that we could become independent and self-sustaining.

He taught me that hard work, excellence and discipline count, and that there's no substitute for hard work, dedication and commitment if you want to achieve your goals. He taught Merle and me to seize every opportunity if a door opened for us and it was something that we really wanted.

Dad taught us to persevere no matter what came our way: this valuable lesson has seen me through some very tough times of my own. He also taught us to always give of our best and to live life to the fullest.

The importance of financial independence was a key part of his messaging to his daughters. From early on he taught me that I should not depend on a man to take care of me. I needed to be financially independent. Given where I come from, the message that I needed to take care of myself financially was very important. I also learnt that I needed to find a partner who wouldn't be affronted by this, and I'm very fortunate to have found such a partner in my husband, Kevin.

Chapter 2

My childhood

My mother was born in St. Monica's Home on 27 November 1937, the first of six children born to Ma and Pa Wyngaard. She had one sister, Joan, and four brothers: Brian, Vicky, Georgie and Charlie. They lived in Heathfield, an area bordered by Retreat to the South and Diep River to the North.

Mum attended St. Anthony's Primary School in Heathfield and then went to St. Augustine's High School in Parow. She had to leave school after she passed Standard 7, to help to support the family. After job-hunting with a few school friends she managed to find a job working in a clothing factory, a job that left her crying every day because of poor working conditions and her fear of the boss.

She later got another job as a clerical worker at Castle Wine and Brandy, where she was taught to use the computer and started to process the statements. Mum worked at Castle Wine for sixteen years until the company was sold to Distillers, who had their own computer staff and she had to find another job. This led her to Reader's Digest as a data capture clerk, and she was soon promoted and put in charge of all refund cheques and customer service on the phone.

Mum was very dedicated to her work. She caught a train to Cape Town station from Retreat every day and walked uphill along Strand Street for at least two kilometres to Reader's Digest. This she did for the next twenty-one years.

When I was growing up, whenever I had a bad day and was scared or worried about something, she would be there for me. She was – and still is – my rock. My mother would comfort me, and her eyes would gleam with a light that spoke of peace, even in the fiercest storm. Her smile would give me hope and the confidence to rise again. Mum's voice would speak so kindly that any fear and anxiety would melt away, and she has been a great inspiration to me throughout my life, especially in the dark moments, when no-one other than my mother could have said the right thing.

My mother taught me the importance of a good work ethic; this has always stood me in good stead. She constantly reminded us that nothing comes easily: we would have to work hard if we wanted to succeed. My parents were determined that we would liberate ourselves from the hand history had dealt us, and make a better life for ourselves.

As I reflect on my own childhood, the key messages that kept coming through are that we needed to continue to educate ourselves. We needed a personal vision, and we needed to ensure that we lived our values. Values like integrity, dignity, fairness and respect for others were drilled into us as children from a very young age. Hard work and discipline featured very prominently in our lives.

The combination of a good education, a strong personal vision and sound values have enabled me to endure extreme hardship, build resilience and ultimately, improve the quality of my life. Our upbringing might not have been easy, but it prepared us for a better life.

My sister Merle and I only lived in our own house over weekends or when my parents were on holiday. My parents both worked long hours, and it wasn't safe to leave young children at home alone without any adult supervision in Steenberg. As a result, during the week, we lived with my grandmother. My parents dropped us off on a Sunday afternoon and we only caught the bus to our own home on Friday afternoon.

I'm very close to my sister, Merle, and we are both similar and very different in many ways. We have a loving family, we get on extremely well and she has been a huge support for me. She'll always stand up for and looks out for me. She's always there for me in whatever way, shape or form that I need her, and she knows that I'm always there for her too.

It's difficult to be objective about what I was like as a child. I can, however, remember being fairly reflective, something of a day-dreamer. I was often smacked for not paying sufficient attention, but I would soon find myself drifting off into a world of my own again. But I do know I'm on very firm ground when I say the foundations for a life of service were cast at a very young age. This isn't surprising given that my parents have always devoted their lives to the service of others.

Mum is very strongly grounded in Christianity and she loves doing good. When she retired she started spending a lot more time at Morea Old Age Home in Louts River, Grassy Park. She recognised that many of the residents are lonely and some may even feel abandoned.

She wants to make the elderly happy, and she does so in a number of ways such as counselling the elderly, listening to their concerns and complaints. She visits them every week and always brings them tea and cake. The elderly folk look forward to my mom's visits, which bring them some laughter and happiness. They sit together and knit or crochet, and my mom sells whatever they make at the local flea market. My parents also organise outings for the elderly, taking them to lunch at the Spur, to the beach or out to celebrate Easter and Christmas with a slap-up meal.

So it's really no surprise that service to the community is part of my make-up. As far back as I can remember, I've always wanted to be 'a little light in the world', even if it is only a little flicker of light.

For me it has always been about who I am and what I am going to do to make a contribution, even if it is only small. Making a contribution doesn't have to be earth-shattering: it can be something as simple as finding a way to make someone feel truly special.

So when I think back about what has motivated me, I can say quite emphatically that it has never been about receiving positive feedback or praise. It was never about recognition. Even today, I just feel good when I do something really well. The need to do things well has always driven me and continues to do so. I need to do an excellent job, and do it with enthusiasm and diligence; provide a service to the best of my ability.

I acknowledge, however, that my parents and my teachers planted some important seeds, including a belief that I had the potential to do something more with my life.

My mother taught me how to live a meaningful life and how to have a dream and make it happen. For her and my father, life was a challenge in many ways and they made sure that we never knew the burden of the pain they must have carried. They taught us to serve and to ask for nothing in return.

In many respects, my mum was very much like her mother, Ma Wyngaard. We had chores, which needed to be done at a certain time, to a certain standard. We had to polish floors, clean windows, run errands, and wash the dishes. No whingeing, back-chatting or excuses were ever tolerated. Time was allocated for chores, homework and play, and we had to be polite and respectful at all times.

Ma Wyngaard, lived in Wyehill Way, Square Hill, Retreat (off Concert Boulevard) which was very close to Square Hill Primary, the school both Merle and I attended. She was an important influence on both Merle and me, especially during our formative years.

She took very good care of us, and we wanted for nothing. I think of her often, and I know that without her strong guiding hand, my life might have turned out quite differently.

My grandmother was a domestic worker for a high-ranking naval officer, Molly Wright, whom we affectionately and respectfully called 'Miss Molly'. Miss Molly lived in a house in Kalk Bay, built right against the mountain. The view from her home was magnificent: you could see the whole of False Bay. Her house was huge and at least ten times the size of ours, or so it seemed at the time.

My grandmother cleaned Miss Molly's house in the morning, and she always made sure that she was home before we returned from school. My grandfather was not well, so she also took care of him between her daily domestic duties and taking care of us before retiring and when his health permitted, Pa Wyngaard worked as a gardener.

Miss Molly had a considerable influence on my grandmother. This may have been where her desire to be English and to be 'prim and proper' came from. The ritual around Miss Molly visiting Ma was both fascinating and terrifying.

We had to dress up in our Sunday best, ensure that our hair was done, our clothing was neatly pressed and our shoes shone. No exceptions. We had to sit quietly with our hands on our lap and we were only allowed to speak when spoken to. We also had to ensure that we spoke our best English and that we were extremely polite. If you giggled or did something you were not supposed to do, you knew as sure as evening gives rise to morning, you would be in a lot of trouble when Miss Molly left.

My granny instilled a rigorous sense of discipline, order and focus in us. She was very organised, and everything had to be done on time. There was a time to play, a time for chores, a time for homework and a time to go to bed. You came home from school, and you washed your socks and your shirt. After all we only had one set of school clothes and they needed to be clean for the next day. You did your homework and you ran errands.

My granny's instructions were always very clear. Food was served on time and play was for a certain amount of time. As much as I used to complain about the discipline at the time, it remains an integral part of my life. I conduct both my personal and business life in a very logical and systematic manner.

What happens during your most impressionable years has a huge impact on your life. I've tried to explain this to my husband. Now, when I do something, he teases me: "You're behaving as though your grandmother was still here today, quality-controlling what to do."

The ritual of always wanting to clear the table and wash the dishes straight after dinner is a case in point. Even today, after so many years, I still find myself needing to clear the table straight after dinner. I need to wash up immediately and pack the dishes away.

Strangely, Kevin's father, Reuben, instilled the same traits in him: a good work ethic, punctuality and precision when going about things. Kevin started his first part-time job at just twelve, when he worked as a petrol pump attendant at his dad's business. Perhaps it was this characteristic that unknowingly attracted me to him.

Ma Wyngaard was quite a task-master. Merle and I had to clean and polish the front stoep (porch). If this wasn't done entirely to her liking, we'd have to do it again. For Ma it was about doing things the right way. If you didn't, you were chastised. It was pointless sulking or feeling sorry for yourself, as no-one would feel sorry for you. You soon learnt to get over it very quickly. This helped me to strive always to do things properly, with total commitment the first time round.

You never dared walk into Ma's house in a pair of wet shoes. Today, I can appreciate why Ma taught us to do this. It's all about being considerate of others. At the time, there seemed to be far too many rules and regulations. As a child, I remember wanting to break as many of them as I could, but I was too terrified to face the wrath of Ma.

While there were lots of chores that needed to be done there was still time for play. I have very fond memories playing in the park across the road from her house. The park with its swings, jungle gym and slide was a magnet for the children in the neighbourhood, and we relished playing outside with our friends. We could not wait to be given the okay to go out. After all the chores and school homework, just one hour of play in the afternoon made our day.

But even when we were playing we were still very much under Ma's control and within her view. She would watch us as we played, and shout out of the window: "Behave yourself! You'll come inside unless you behave." Behaving appropriately was a pivotal part of our upbringing.

But it wasn't just my granny who checked our behaviour. The parents in the neighbourhood would set you straight for bad behaviour, and if you behaved very badly, you earned a smack. That aunt or uncle would certainly report the misdemeanour to your parents for further punishment. Back then, your neighbours, your school, your church and the sport club you played for all instilled the same good values and behaviour expected of you; they were the extension of your community and it was acceptable to your parents that they had the right to chastise you for misbehaviour.

When Ma felt that we had played for long enough she'd call us inside. The other children, who ran wild and ran free, would ask: "Shirley, why must you go?" We knew that if Ma said we must go, that was the end of it.

My granny was always very protective and if there was even the slightest hint of rain, much to our friends' delight, she'd make us wear our raincoat and Wellington boots. Our friends teased us relentlessly. When I thought I was out of sight, I'd take off my raincoat and my Wellingtons, to avoid the teasing. But we soon learnt that we never got away with anything. If anyone had eyes at the back of their head, it was Ma. She'd be waiting for me when I returned from school. "Shirley, I saw you remove your raincoat before you got to the bottom of the road. Why did you do that when I told you to keep it on?"

Thinking back, I sometimes become angry and think she was too hard on us. Being the eldest, I felt the full brunt of this as I was always supposed to know better. I had to make sure that my younger sister walked home from school with me, but also had to make sure that she never got hurt at school. If Merle got hurt then I had to explain and bear the related consequences. This was a lot of responsibility for a young girl.

Some errands for my granny meant catching a train to Kalk Bay to buy fresh fish right off the fishing boats. On other occasions, it meant delivering a package to Miss Molly. Because I was given quite a lot of responsibility, I became streetwise as a young girl, learning very quickly how to take care of myself. Many of the other children played all afternoon and did not have any responsibility to speak of.

She taught me how to pick fruit and to make the most delicious fig jam, and about buying bread and meat and doing the daily shopping for the family. Check the colour of the meat and texture of the bread for freshness. Look carefully for sell-by dates: the best bargains may not be the best bargain because it's no longer good to eat. She'd make a list and always wrote the price next to each item. This was invaluable as it taught me to do the maths, and I also learnt to check that the change was correct.

Like the rest of us my granny had her flaws and her prejudices. She made life very difficult for my mum and dad when they were courting. She wasn't convinced Dad would make a good husband. Besides, he was too dark of complexion for Ma's liking.

She also had prejudices about Afrikaans, and about the company we kept. You were not allowed to speak Afrikaans in her house, and you weren't allowed to bring certain friends home, because they weren't good enough. We couldn't understand her prejudices as children, and would often cringe: "Why is she doing this to me?"

There's no denying that apartheid messed with people's heads. Lives were modelled around stereotypes and prejudices. Even as a child, with a Christian upbringing, I knew this had to be wrong. How could there be a God who created us all and then you decide that you cannot spend time with people because they speak Afrikaans, or because they are too dark in complexion?

It was a very strange world to navigate. I thought a lot about these anomalies as a child, and none of it made any sense: racism, prejudice, stereotyping must be wrong. One thing was certain: I knew I'd do things differently when I grew up.

Ma Wyngaard eventually moved in with us. By this time we'd moved to another house in Grassy Park. I remember Ma complaining one morning that her legs were very sore. I said: "Ma, walk, you'll be fine." I dropped her off at Aunty Joan's house on my way to school. Aunty Joan, my Mom's sister and my Godmother, rang the school where I taught at a few minutes later announcing that Ma had suffered a stroke and was being taken to hospital.

Although Ma was discharged, the stroke was severe and she needed a lot of nursing. She had always taken such good care of us and now it was our turn to take care of her. My daily watch was the 10pm to 2am shift. But that day, when I went to my room at the end of my watch, my dad called soon afterwards to say that Ma had just passed away.

Ma will always be very special to me. She was our family matriarch; she was much larger than life. After all of these years, she remains a huge presence, even in death. She left a lasting impression on our lives. We still speak of her as though she was still alive. We still joke with great fondness about her many eccentricities, including the fact that she believed she had royal blood coursing through her veins.

Chapter 3

My Education

I had what was typically called a 'gutter education' i.e. segregated education for blacks.

The 1953 Bantu Education Act was one of apartheid's most offensively racist laws. Bantu education was designed to teach African pupils to be "hewers of wood and drawers of water" for a white-run economy and society, regardless of an individual's abilities and aspirations. In what are now infamous words, Minster of Native Affairs, Dr. Hendrik F. Verwoerd, explained the government's new education policy to the South African Parliament:

> "There is no space for him [the "Native"] in the European Community above certain forms of labour. For this reason it is of no avail for him to receive training which has its aim in the absorption of the European Community, where he cannot be absorbed. Until now he has been subjected to a school system which drew him away from his community and misled him by showing him the greener pastures of European Society where he is not allowed to graze." (Kallaway, 1984)

It was an education designed to ensure that you didn't succeed in life in general, never mind a career, and that you continued to accept the oppression that you faced. It was one of apartheid's strongest measures, ensuring that the vast majority of the population were educated just enough to provide an unskilled, cheap labour force for the country, but no more than that.

Merle, who was far more playful than me, sailed through school easily and with great success. Many people are surprised to learn that I wasn't a straight-A student; I only obtained my first distinction much later in life – when I did my postgraduate studies. I had to work much harder to achieve my academic goals, and I studied as conscientiously as I could to get good results. Nevertheless, I loved school and I'm still in close contact with many of my friends from primary and high school who continue to be my pillars of support today.

But it wasn't an easy journey for me. I vividly recall an incident in Sub A where my teacher reprimanded me. We were learning to write the letters of the alphabet, and had to write them on a straight line. She looked at my work, and then she took a purple crayon and drew a big X across my page. She said: "This isn't good enough. Start again." I was devastated and didn't know what to do, so I burst into tears. I learnt very quickly that excellence needed to become a habit.

There were some teachers that I really connected to, though. My best friend, Renae Barker-Clay, who's been my friend since we were six, reminds me that I was a bit of a teacher's pet, as the teacher always asked me to make her a cup of tea during break. But for me this wasn't simply a transactional relationship between teacher and learner – there was a real connection. There was a sense of her treating me in a way that said, "I value you. You're a great kid. You have a lot of potential."

By the time I reached matric, many of my teachers were verbalising this. There was a sense of: "Although you don't get straight As, you have the self-discipline. You know what hard work is all about. You apply yourself. You really try hard. These are elements that can take you forward into university. You have the potential to do so much more." Renae, Tracey Arendse and I were great friends at high School (known as the three musketeers) shared our dreams for the future with each other.

My high school was South Peninsula High School in Diep River, Cape Town. In terms of the Group Areas Act, it was a coloured school situated in a white area, which caused all kinds of problems. The authorities tried to close down the school throughout the 1960s, but families fought hard to keep it open. When I enrolled in the mid-1970s I was told that the school might still close.

Attending South Peninsula High School came with its own set of challenges. Pupils were only allowed to walk down one road to gain access to the school: Francis Road. We were told that if there were any complaints from people living in this street we could be suspended, or even arrested.

Our teachers were very mindful of the educational, political and social dynamics of the time. Even though certain books and some conversations were banned, we read these and we had these conversations nevertheless.

I was in Standard 7 when the Soweto uprising broke out in 1976. Police descended on our school and started beating up people. This context fired up my personal mission for justice and equality in our time.

The teachers at South Peninsula High were truly inspiring. They pushed their pupils hard, academically, gave recognition (and sanction, where required) when we made progress in specific subjects, and they took pride in our achievements.

At least two of my teachers – Mr Brian Isaacs and Mr Riyaadh Najaar – thought I had university potential, and they encouraged me to go home and discuss with my parents the possibility of my attending university – and for that I will always be grateful.

Mr Isaacs, my Biology teacher, who is now principal of South Peninsula High, wrote in my little autograph book when I was in matric in 1979, "Always aim high, and you will inevitably succeed." Mr Najaar, now the principal at Spine Road High, wrote, "You have the attributes to make a success of anything you attempt." These words at that time of my life had a significant impact on the choices I made and the path I took after matric.

This was a major turning point for me – university wasn't an automatic progression for children who grew up on the Cape Flats. It still isn't.

My parents wanted me to complete my matric so that I could find a job and assist the family financially. This was the aspiration. This was the big goal. Obtaining a matric certificate was (and still is) a key milestone and is a requisite for entry to most forms of employment, or, better still, the possibility of a tertiary education. So I really worked hard at my studies, so as not to disappoint my parents, but also because I knew that if I passed well, my future prospects would be so much better.

During my matric year I sat down with my parents and discussed my dreams of pursuing a tertiary education. Understandably, they were concerned about how I would raise the money to do so.

But I obtained a university exemption and was able to obtain a government bursary to study teaching. In 1980 I enrolled at the University of the Western Cape (UWC) for a BA degree, majoring in English, Latin and Sociology. Teaching isn't necessarily the career I would've chosen for myself at the time; I would far rather have studied law.

I learnt early in life to be pragmatic and rational and I realised that the only way that I'd be able to further my education was to apply for a bursary to become a teacher. I saw teaching as a building block to a possible future where I'd be able to choose what I really wanted to do. (So use the opportunities presented to you, even if they are stepping-stones to the next audacious milestone.)

Many remember the heady, fun-filled, carefree days of university; my university days were nothing like this. University life was not about being ensconced in some safe, academic, ivory tower: it was a time of bitter, violent, political struggle.

In the 1980s universities were a cauldron of political dissent and students were at the heart of the struggle against oppression. My dearest friend at UWC, Dr Anita Maurtin-Cairncross, and I worked hard on our academic studies and weathered many storms of student life as we started off as bright-eyed, bushy-tailed first year students in 1980. Our lecturers told us that by the end of the first semester in first year, half of the students would not be in the class any more as they would not have made the grade. We were determined to pass.

The fact that universities were designated for specific race groups illustrates the deep schisms in society at the time. Located in Bellville in the Western Cape, the UWC was established in 1960 as a university for coloured people only.

The university was rife with student protest against apartheid. Many students at the university supported the black consciousness movement; several student leaders became prominent activists in organisations such as the United Democratic Front (UDF). I joined the UDF in the early 1980s, and in 1982, the university rejected the apartheid ideology formally in its mission statement.

My first year as a student at UWC, 1980, coincided with the second uprising in education. The campus was literally on fire. I vividly recall dodging brutal, baton-wielding police on campus, which was a terrifying experience.

That year was particularly challenging as far as education in South Africa was concerned. There were massive school and university boycotts, and a huge crisis erupted: black South African students protested over the so-called 'Bantu' education, which had expressly been designed for black people and was aimed at keeping them ignorant and subservient.

The continued unrest was linked to labour strikes, rate-payers' association strikes, and international sanctions. Security forces within the apartheid government tried to control the upheavals by force and this led to serious confrontations, injury and death for many in their fight for democracy in South Africa.

I quickly started to develop a socio-political consciousness, which led me to understand why the inhabitants of the neighbourhoods or townships I grew up in were now so vociferous about the socio-economic plight of blacks. I also realised that there were deep ideological underpinnings to apartheid that needed to be exposed.

My first year at UWC was fairly chaotic, as there were very few classes running, given the nationwide challenges in education. My student debts were also mounting. Things started going downhill very badly in May 1980. During a serious discussion with my parents we came to the conclusion that I should rather find a job. A lot of money was being spent to educate me and I wasn't even attending classes. Worse still, I might get hurt in the unrest on campus.

Reluctantly, I cancelled my registration in May, wondering whether I'd ever be able to realise my dream of furthering my education. Often I had to wipe away tears and put on a brave face as I prepared for interviews with prospective employers.

I spent three months looking for work, without any success. There weren't too many jobs going, and searching for employment proved an excruciating and futile exercise.

By September 1980 things had calmed down at UWC, but the campus was in tatters and had suffered the full brunt of student unrest and brutal police retaliation. There hadn't been any lectures for months and some people had lost their lives in the process. I decided, nevertheless, to return to UWC to finish my first year.

I went to the university and asked the registrar to reinstate my registration, and was told to come back the following year. I said: "No, this year." They then asked who would pay for my studies since I had cancelled my bursary when I cancelled my registration. I told them I'd ask the Education Department to reinstate my bursary.

I was as tenacious as a bull terrier. I was not going to give up. Although it took some doing to be re-accepted at the university and to get my bursary reinstated, I wouldn't take no for an answer. I was very fortunate and also very persuasive, and succeeded on both counts. This experience taught me that the impossible is indeed possible, and that one should never ever give up.

Finally enrolled, and with my bursary reinstated, I focused on catching up on my coursework. A lot of blood, sweat and tears, and hours of hard work paid off: I passed my first year and never looked back.

I completed my BA degree in 1982 and went on to complete my Higher Education Diploma in 1983. Money was very tight during my student years. Like many other students I had to work part-time to fund my studies, so I spent weekends working as a cashier at various stores, including Pick 'n Pay and Melotronics, a sound and vision store in Athlone, Cape Town. The value of part-time weekend work must not be underestimated. It taught me discipline and how to manage my finances diligently.

Other part-time work included a few aerobics classes in my spare time. I was super fit then and absolutely loved teaching aerobics. At times I was able to teach up to three classes back-to-back if required to do so.

The discipline that I learnt at this time has stood me in good stead. I learnt that if you want something badly enough, if you're willing to do what it takes, if you're prepared to swim upstream when called upon to do so, what seems impossible is actually possible.

In 1984, I began teaching English at Groenvlei Secondary School, in Lansdowne in the Cape Flats, to fulfil my bursary requirements, which meant four years of teaching in government schools to pay off my bursary.

Being a teacher is a wonderful, uplifting experience, but teaching children who live in historically disadvantaged parts of the Cape Flats is not for the faint-hearted.

I taught children aged between thirteen and eighteen, who came from very challenging backgrounds. There were childhood pregnancies, and drugs, guns and knives were brought to school. Fights between gang members broke out during break time. It's still chilling thinking about this so many years later.

The most depressing part is that very little has changed for the children living on the Cape Flats. Despite all of this, Groenvlei Secondary still produced amazing academic results during those years.

Despite these challenges, as a young teacher I had an opportunity to help and also inspire my pupils. If I were teaching Shakespeare, I'd try to make Shakespeare relevant for them. I made them read Shakespeare bearing in mind that the plays included romance, death, rivalry, betrayal, love, and hate. We'd talk about this and relate it back to their lives.

The children's struggles resonated with me because I knew where they came from and I was able to relate to their personal circumstances. In addition to teaching them English, I tried to strengthen their emotional resolve and to teach them that if they made a decision they needed to stick with this no matter what. This was critical if they were to improve their own personal circumstances and succeed in life.

Since there was a lot of peer pressure, it was important never to allow others to talk them out of things easily. I told them constantly that the starting point for their lives was to ensure that they never made poor decisions, because those decisions would have consequences.

The 1980s were very difficult years for South Africa as the struggle to break the back of apartheid intensified. In July 1985 the South African government declared a state of emergency in parts of the country affected by the unrest. During this period many activists were put on trial, detainees had limited rights, the press was restricted and public gatherings were restricted.

In the run-up to the tenth anniversary of the Soweto riots, around two thousand people were arrested and the government tried to curb the unrest by imposing a nationwide state of emergency. It was during this period that the UDF was banned.

I learnt to build relationships with the community and with parents. There were times when the teachers had to ferret some of the children out of hospitals. I had to speak to parents about their child being detained during the protest march outside the school, or about their child being beaten up badly by the police. Some children were too scared to go home because the police might find them. In these instances we had to make a plan to ensure their safety.

It was a huge learning curve for me when I realised how intricately education was linked to political, social and economic policies and how important principled decisions would be if we were to fundamentally change the state of education in our country.

I became active in various campaigns to eradicate racism and sexism in education. As I recall, in 1985, part of the strategy to bring 'order' back to schools was to enforce a final examination in a year when there had been huge disruptions to learning and teaching. The thought of being required to do this, when our schools were constantly being invaded by gun-wielding police, was unimaginable.

The teachers at Groenvlei decided to take a stand on this vital educational principle: we could not administer an examination if our pupils had not been to school and had lessons. We would not do this because our pupils had been brutalised by police during this time.

We were advised by the education department that we were in breach of our employment contracts and would be suspended if we did not follow their directives. That made me realise just how important values and principles are, but also what dire consequences awaited us in this scenario: we could lose our jobs.

Chapter 4

"We shall overcome"

If I remember correctly, there were seventy-two teachers in the Western Cape who took this stance. When the first case went to court, the teachers won based on sound educational and legal principles: pupils had to be taught a piece of work before they could be examined on it. As soon as the case was officially withdrawn against all the teachers we went back to our schools, to catch up on the work lost and get back to the business of educating children.

In spite of the uprisings, I decided to pursue post-graduate studies through Unisa, and completed an honours degree in education on a part-time basis. I knew with absolute certainty that education would liberate me from the shackles of poverty and unemployment. I knew I had to show determination, discipline, dedication and most of all, work very hard, to transcend the hardships of the socio-economic challenges that I confronted.

We used to sing struggle songs, like "We shall overcome," with such conviction. I firmly believed that we would overcome, and my resolve grew as did my determination to make a difference.

I joined the Teachers' League of South Africa (TLSA), whose motto was: 'Let us live for our children.' The TLSA, established in 1931, had emerged in response to increasing racial segregation in Cape Town schools. The league advocated non-racism and equality, and I was keen to learn from these well-respected and seasoned teachers how we could advance this agenda in education.

On a personal front, in 1985 I bought my very first house in Grassy Park, with the staggering mortgage of R85 000. I was so proud of my tiny house, which represented a whole new beginning for me.

However, just one month after moving into that house I was told that our group of teachers would be suspended for not following the education department's directives over the final exams. The likelihood of being dismissed naturally caused me great distress, but I was prepared to face the worst, as I believed in the justness of the principles and values we espoused.

To earn extra money, I taught matric English in Lansdowne, at Savio Adult Education College, an adult education institution that enabled adults to complete their matric by attending classes after hours. I taught there two nights a week for about five years. The students came from a wide range of backgrounds, filing into class after a full day's work to prepare for those crucial exams.

My oldest pupil was a former headmaster, who although retired, wanted to complete his matric. I had to find a way to teach the adults in my class Shakespeare and poetry in a way that could be understood across generational diversity, and I had to find a way to get them to pass their matric. Their courage and determination inspired me to really go out of my way to help them to succeed.

During the remaining week nights I taught aerobics classes at the Athlone Technikon and Pat's Gym in Grassy Park, to raise sufficient funds to pay my bond and living expenses. I've always loved sport, and as a child, I participated in various activities such as the 100m, 200m and relay sprints at school events.

Kevin has, in more recent years, encouraged me to start running half-marathons. This is something that I thought was impossible for me to do. But Kevin has an amazing positive influence over people – he's able to inspire them to excel, and he hardly ever takes no for an answer.

For example, in 2004 he encouraged a friend born with dwarfism, to start running. Simon Mamadi thought his disability made it impossible for him to complete a five kilometre fun run at the time, but with dedicated training sessions with Kevin he grew strong and built up stamina. In 2007 he finished the Two Oceans half-marathon to a standing ovation. It was a heart-wrenching finish with Kevin and Simon managing to cross the finish line as the very two last runners to receive a medal before the cut-off time period of three hours. And again, the impossible is possible.

I started small and ramped up my efforts, running before or after work and over weekends. Also realising how much it improved my health and overall well-being, I was determined to run my first half-marathon. In April 2015, I completed my seventh Two Oceans half-marathon.

One of the athletic pursuits I loved at school was dancing. I'd developed a passion for dancing at an early age, starting ballet lessons in the community hall on Concert Boulevard in Retreat, Cape Town, when I was about six. I enjoyed ballet classes till I was in matric.

Dance and ballet taught me discipline: I learnt that practice, determination and dedication are vital to pulling off a great performance. Our ballet class took part in concerts at various Cape Town schools, and after matric I ventured into other dance genres such as ballroom and a bit of Cape Town jazz. Terrance Wanneberg has to be mentioned for being a great dance partner, even to this day.

The best jazz club in Cape Town was Club Galaxy in Rylands Estate where we went every Thursday evening and Saturday afternoon. We loved the jazz played by bands like N2, Tony Schilder and Airborne, and of course, DJ Keith, DJ Mark Johnson, and DJ Brian "Bo" Horne were awesome. Club Galaxy attracted an array of talented dancers who moved with so much enthusiasm and passion that you simply had to join in. Kevin and I also enjoy ballroom dancing, and while we're not the most expert ballroom dancers, we take our chances. We go to a few ballroom dances, better known as "langarm" occasionally, and enjoy the live bands like Les Versatiles, Ikey Gamba and Bobby Hendricks.

I love the musicality, the fluidity and the beauty of dance. I love the way that dance can liberate your soul when you cross over from the sheer physical, practised movement, to an indescribable, amazing sensation of deep alignment. It transcends intellectual, cognitive processing and takes you to a higher level of being.

And it meant that teaching aerobics was a good way for me to earn some extra money – it came pretty naturally to me. As you can imagine, it also kept me very fit, especially since I often gave several classes a day. These were tough times, but all that hard work and effort formed the building blocks to a life of even greater complexity and prepared me for the challenges to come.

Having completed the requisite four years as a teacher in December 1987, I joined UWC's Faculty of Education as a senior language laboratory assistant. Fully aware that education would liberate me from poverty, enhance my quality of life, and also enable me to have a positive impact on the lives of others, I decided to forge ahead with my own studies at the same time. It was during this time that I met Kevin, never imagining we would someday be married. It feels as though I've always known Kevin.

I knew him for many years before we became romantically involved: we actually met while at high school. We went to two competing schools (he went to Livingstone High), but both schools were known for being great at sport and academic performance.

Kevin was known as a good sportsman and middle-distance runner. He played for and was a founder member of many sport clubs, and he became well-known as a schools sport administrator when he was teaching in the 1980s. Kevin was a Physical Education teacher at York Road Primary. The school was located next to Groenvlei High, where I had taught, and our paths inevitably crossed during this period.

When Kevin attended some of my aerobics classes in Athlone, I took note. And our paths crossed again at UWC in 1988, as Kevin had returned to UWC to complete a degree in Human Movement Sciences.

But it took years for us to take a real interest in each other. So often we met in passing at social events, but never really interacted with each other. And while we played squash for different clubs – Kevin for Trojans, and I for Victoria – we very often played our games at the same squash venue.

We'd say hello as we passed each other at squash, and then in January 1988, when I got the job at UWC, and Kevin had enrolled to finish his degree, one day he walked past my office, and we started to chat about what each of us was doing at UWC. "Now I know where to find you for a cup of coffee," Kevin said.

It was very hot that summer, and I used to go to the pool to cool off, but I couldn't swim, so I just sort of jumped around in the pool. When I thought that nobody was really looking I attempted to swim. All the Physical Education students were there, and Kevin was assigned to teach first year students to learn to swim. He was a swimming coach and life-saver.

One day one of his friends, Nigel Davids, jokingly pointed me out and said, "It looks like that girl needs help, Mr Zinn!" So Kevin started teaching me the basics, and that was the beginning and the end of my swimming lessons! And our relationship just developed from there over time. However, I can swim somewhat today.

By the time Kevin and I became properly romantically involved that year, I'd signed up for a scholarship to Italy to complete a Master's degree. As I had majored in Latin, this was a very exciting opportunity. All my documentation had been approved by the Italian Consulate and everything was ready for me to leave. And then Kevin said: "Please, you really don't have to go. If you want to travel, we can travel together." He'd already travelled overseas, and he promised that if I remained in South Africa, he'd take me overseas someday.

He was very persuasive. I'd invested emotionally in our relationship, so I cancelled my arrangements and started a Master's in Education at the University of the Western Cape. I believed I'd found someone who would make a wonderful life partner. And he was true to his word: towards the end of that year Kevin and I travelled overseas.

We bought Delta passes, which enabled us to fly into as many cities as we could in the US in a one-month period on Delta Airlines. We eventually went to Rome and we also saw a bit of the rest of Italy. Today we still love to travel to off-the-beaten track places, and Kevin has always delivered on his promises to me.

Chapter 5

Harvard beckons

Kevin's mom, Jean, is an avid newspaper reader. When we visited her one evening she handed me a small notice that she'd cut out of the newspaper, calling for applications for the Harvard South African Fellowship. The fellowship, which had by then been awarded just six times since 1979, was intended for mid-career South Africans who had been disadvantaged under apartheid.

Offering to fund the successful applicant's Harvard studies for a full academic year, it not only made provision for the payment of all tuition for the full period of enrolment, it also sponsored a full round-trip airfare between South Africa and Boston. A monthly stipend would cover the cost of housing and living expenses. I was acutely aware that barely a few years before, no-one would have thought such an amazing opportunity would be possible – certainly not in our lifetime.

I showed Kevin the advertisement and explained to him that it was an opportunity for us to combine travel and study. I never gave any thought to the very fierce competition I'd face from other applicants. It was a shot in the dark, and I never expected anything to come of it, but I couldn't help thinking how wonderful it would be if I were accepted.

Kevin and my family encouraged me to give it a shot, so I took the plunge and submitted my application. To my great surprise I was invited to an interview in Johannesburg. A formidable panel, comprising Harvard South African Fellowship alumni, Harvard alumni and the Committee of African Studies Faculty Chair, interviewed the short-listed candidates.

I was terribly nervous and overwhelmed during the interview, but I knew deep down that I really was keen on this, so I focused my mind on being successful and answered their questions to the very best of my ability. By the end of the interview, I was emotionally drained. It was very difficult to gauge how the interview had gone, but whatever the outcome, I was grateful that I'd at least been invited to an interview.

To my very pleasant surprise I learnt a few weeks later that I'd been accepted. I had to prepare to leave, as their academic year started in September 1990. I'd only finished my Masters through UWC in August 1990.

When I received the letter confirming my selection as a Harvard Fellow, I was thrilled beyond belief. I was accepted at the Harvard Graduate School of Education, and I began my second Master's in Education in September 1990, having taken a year's study leave from UWC.

Kevin and I had been together for about two years and were happily living together. There had been a bit of a fall-out with my family, with my dad in particular, as he disapproved of our live-in arrangement, and this made things very difficult, especially for Kevin. But we lived apart while I was in Boston. Kevin moved in with his friend, Andre Steenkamp, and continued teaching at UWC.

The learning experience at Harvard gave me a new perspective, and the relationships I forged with other students and teaching staff were priceless. Being at Harvard was like being a child in a candy store. There were so many interesting things to do.

I was surrounded by the most inspiring academics, and they all encouraged me to consider pursuing a doctorate at Harvard. The competition to get into the doctoral programme is extremely fierce: applicants face global competition, and the standards are incredibly high. The mere thought of what was required made me shudder; it was very daunting. However, the seeds of encouragement had started to grow within me, and I started contemplating this option very seriously. I also learned that surrounding yourself with people who inspire and uplift you is very important.

The Master's programme was a nine-month course-work programme, and I graduated in June 1991. By then I had been convinced to give the doctorate a go, and I started the process of applying for entry to the doctoral programme. I knew I would have to overcome many obstacles. First, how would I pay for it? Second, a doctorate would take several years to complete. How was I going to manage this? Thirdly, I was obliged to return to UWC, as I had only received one year's study leave to complete my Master's.

Kevin and I had maintained a long-distance relationship during the year that I was completing my Master's, but it was very difficult, and our relationship was taking serious strain. Long-distance relationships have their complexities and when your international telephone bills arrive, and the emotional gap is stretched, you need a lot of staying power.

We'd agreed that we were going to do this and that we'd still be together when the year was over, but it was quite another thing actually doing it. I was so immersed in my studies at Harvard that I had very little time for anything else.

The geographical distance is bad enough, but there are other distances that this kind of situation puts between two people. There were a lot of questions: should we give up? Is this going to work into the future? Should we find other partners? These were the kind of conversations we were having, and it wasn't easy.

But nothing is ever too much trouble for Kevin, even the entire rigmarole of visiting me in Boston. We set a date, and agreed that it would be cheaper if I bought the ticket in Boston and couriered it to Cape Town. I used the little bit of extra money that I had to buy Kevin a ticket at the Harvard Square Travel Centre. It was the cheapest ticket I could find, and it would take him first to Tel Aviv and then to Boston.

Of course, it didn't go quite as planned – there were nail-biting delays with the courier who had to deliver the ticket to Kevin in Cape Town. Our frustration and anxiety grew exponentially: I had bought a ticket that could not be changed – and it would see him flying through Tel Aviv just as the Gulf War broke out in 1991.

The ticket arrived in Cape Town literally on the day of his departure, and when he landed in Israel, he was frog-marched around the airport in Tel Aviv, but fortunately he managed to get to Boston. However, we had to change the ticket for his return as it was not possible to travel back along this route.

During his visit we discussed how to move forward if I did a doctorate and he joined me in the US. We both felt uncertain – we'd been apart for a whole year, so it was a difficult decision to make. However, eventually we decided together that I should pursue my studies, so I applied to be allowed into the doctoral programme.

And I got in! Having gone through all the interviews, the presentations and the motivation, I had actually been accepted onto the doctoral programme at Harvard. I was beginning to see that hard work and excellence are key to success. Hard work is not enough on its own, though. You have to excel in everything you do, regardless of the challenges and setbacks.

But there was one more, rather serious obstacle to overcome. Harvard had accepted me, but UWC turned down my leave application. I really wanted to continue with the momentum my Master's had generated. It had been such an experience, and I was so excited to have been accepted. And having jumped through all of those hoops, now it seemed that I couldn't continue because UWC wouldn't grant me any more leave.

I was frustrated and a little angry. I felt it was unreasonable that some of my colleagues were being allowed time off to do all kinds of things, while I was getting all this uphill. I realise now that I was a bit of a problem for UWC, because I challenged all of their justifications. I think I was ... a bit of a pain ... in the butt.

Nobody defers a doctorate at Harvard. It just isn't done. But UWC wanted me to work for another year, at which point they would review whether or not to grant me another year's study leave. I worked that year, but they still refused to grant me further leave, so I asked for unpaid leave. They reminded me that a doctorate takes anything between five and seven years to complete; they also raised the point that on completion I might not return to the university.

I told them I wanted to make that choice once I'd completed the doctorate, not before. All that I was asking for was an opportunity to complete my doctorate at Harvard.

My leave wasn't approved, so I did something that I wouldn't normally do: I approached Rhoda Kadalie, the gender commissioner at the university, for assistance. I told her what a wonderful experience completing my Master's at Harvard had been, how much support I'd received, and how excited I was to have been accepted onto their doctoral programme. I realised that I could complete a doctorate through the University of the Western Cape as a faculty member, but very few people actually get the opportunity to complete a doctorate at Harvard, so I was determined to seize this opportunity with both hands. Rhoda said we'd have a conversation at the next Senate meeting.

My first observation was that the room was filled with men: there weren't any other women in the room. The Chair asked: "Are you Shirley Zinn?" I replied that I was. He said Rhoda hadn't been invited and asked her to leave. She explained that she was representing my case. The Chair said she could stay, but she wasn't allowed to speak. I had to speak for myself.

Only one or two of the people in the room supported me – it was a very difficult discussion. They eventually gave me one year's unpaid leave, after which I had to return to the university. I accepted the offer, but I knew this was impossible.

On a personal level, things were also in a bit of turmoil, as Kevin and I had to decide whether or not we had a future together. Having a long-distance relationship had been tough, and when I came back in June 1991 after my Master's, I honestly didn't know what the future held. But we got ourselves back together again, and now I was considering the doctorate.

I was twenty-seven years old when Kevin and I first became an item. The amazing thing was that we'd been together for four years and were happily in love. We didn't think marriage was quite the institution it could be, so I didn't expect to get married. I was in my early thirties – which is on the shelf by Cape Town standards – and I had no real expectations around marriage. I remember looking at my peers, many of whom had been married for about five years, and they didn't look very happy. I was with someone who was important to me, and that was enough. I suppose I'd lost a little confidence in the institution.

And then one day Kevin came home and said he was feeling rebellious. Maybe we should just do it. And I said, "Are you sure?" And he said, "Ja, let's do it." And that was that. We've never really fitted the mould. The next day he spoke to my dad, and then went to check the available dates at the Wynberg Magistrate's Court. The first date was in two weeks' time at 2pm on a Wednesday, so he booked us a slot for 24 June 1992.

In my family, it was a bit of an odd thing to do. I know my parents would have preferred a traditional church wedding, but decided to come to court nevertheless – their first court wedding ever. It was a bit unnerving for them, perhaps even disappointing, but they supported us. And ten years later we renewed our vows in a church.

Our wedding happened on a cold and very wet day in Cape Town. The plan was to go to court at 2pm, and then have a small dinner at a restaurant in Diep River, as we could only afford to invite immediate family (about ten people) to any kind of reception. So we told a few friends, colleagues and other family members to come across to Kevin's parents' house for a drink after 8pm, expecting a smallish crowd, given the wintry conditions. And I kid you not: about a hundred people showed up. Every time the doorbell rang, Kevin and I rolled our eyes in amazement and concern. The house neither had the capacity to entertain so many people, nor had we prepared snacks for so many.

There were people squeezed into every room of the Kevin's parents' home in Lansdowne: the toilet, the bathroom and the little pantry. With so many people and so much noise and laughter it was impossible to even say a word of thanks. Besides, the guest of honour tasked to make the speech, Andre Steenkamp, was the only guest who got the address wrong and waited for hours outside our Grassy Park home, a home so small, it could barely entertain half a dozen people.

Over at my in-laws' house, I've no idea how they managed to provide food and drinks for so many people. But Kevin's mom, Jean, and her sisters joined forces and cooked up a few pots of food and made snacks to feed the guests.

Jean and I have laughed about this many times – it had to be a miracle. The last person left at 5am the following morning, and despite all the celebration and lack of sleep we had to go work that morning as we still had one day left of the school term. Kevin went from the reception party directly to school. The principal and school staff all enjoyed a good laugh at the state he was in. Fortunately, neither of us was required to teach on that day.

Ours wasn't a lavish wedding – it was a simple affair, with all the legal formalities concluded in a few minutes at the court, and my sister and Kevin's cousin, Russell, as witnesses. But it was no less special to us. We were so grateful for the support of family and friends, and often look fondly at the photos and think about how this all came about.

Kevin is an integral part of my story, because I know that if I had chosen the wrong partner, my life might have turned out very differently. I'm very aware that not everyone is as lucky as I am, and the divorce rates tell their own story. And twenty-three years later, I can say with absolute honesty and conviction that I could not have made a better choice.

Whenever I speak at events I always tell women to honour the men who've made a difference in their lives. It's so easy to say men have been oppressive, or have been barriers to women's development, but there are also many men who've never received the recognition they deserve for being instrumental in our own success: people like my dad, Kevin, and the other men who've done so much to support me.

If it weren't for Kevin, I wouldn't be half the person I am today. He's been incredibly supportive. He's played a key role in my career in terms of providing emotional support and propelling me forward every step of the way. He's had a huge influence on my decision-making.

Through all my career decisions, my studies and my geographical moves, he's always been prepared to do whatever it takes to keep himself busy, stay productive, and continue to try and get into the job market again, when moving to enhance my career has required him to resign from his school teaching position. I really admire that.

He's also stayed with me through everything – through the tough times, and those times when we've been forced to swim upstream. It comes back to those marital vows: "in sickness and in health, for better or for worse". We've certainly been through the mill and Kevin has been firmly at my side through every storm.

He hates the formal parties, corporate functions and events that we have to attend as part of my job. He loathes making small talk with complete strangers, but he accompanies me without grumbling, because he knows it's important to me. We've always given each other space to do the things we love doing, and we've always supported one another. If his job requires him to go away for a day or two to do some anti-doping sport testing, I'll join him if at all possible. If I can't join him, we manage.

We've always done that. We've always understood that it's not the being together every day that makes us successful as a couple; it's about setting each other free to do the things that we love and enjoy and are passionate about. So we can't always be together, but we always check in to see that we're both okay and taking care of ourselves.

I'm often invited to events and weekends away, and one of my previous PAs knew that I liked to include Kevin. She'd always ask: "Can Kevin join Shirley? She'd prefer that." This would sometimes put people in an awkward position, but most often they'd say, "We don't have an extra space at the table, but if Shirley will come along, we'll make provision."

There's never been any traditional division of labour in our home: whoever is available does what needs to be done, whether it's doing the dishes, cleaning windows, doing the shopping, or changing nappies. There's never been any discussion about it. If you see something needs to be done, you get it done. If you can't get it done you have a discussion about it, so you know who'll be able to do this or that, and by when. There are no hard and fast rules. It's a matter of ensuring that it gets done. The same applies to cooking a meal or paying a bill.

Our relationship isn't perfect by any stretch of the imagination, but then no relationship is. What's important is that there is a true meeting of minds on the key issues around our collective lives, and how we best live that together. We give each other the opportunities to be the very best that we can be in our own right.

Ours is a partnership of equals. We have serious differences of opinion around many issues including religious, cultural and socio-political issues. We differ on how we respond to what's happening in South Africa, and in the world in general.

There are spaces where we agree to disagree; there are also spaces where we're both disgruntled. There are times when we get angry and there are times when we'd like decisions to have been made differently. What's important is that while we may not agree on these issues, we respect each other's views, and we also respect each other's right to differ.

We recently had an incident on a Sunday evening where Kevin spontaneously invited some friends we hadn't seen in a while for dinner. I reminded him that I was doing a presentation the next day and needed to prepare. It was five o'clock in the afternoon, and our guests were arriving at six o'clock. Supportive as always, Kevin said: "Why don't you just go and finish and I'll cook the dinner. Have I ever let you down?"

By the time I'd emailed my presentation, our guests were at our front door, and the meal was prepared. It was a glorious evening and we all had a good time. It may not be the relationship everyone else has, but it works for us.

Chapter 6

Times get tough

Our Harvard adventure – together, this time – began in July 1993. This meant a great deal of upheaval for Kevin: he had to give up his job, sell a lot of his favourite possessions, and move halfway across the world. I didn't take this lightly – I will always be grateful to him for the sacrifices he's made.

And the first few months were really tough. The rigour of doing a doctorate was incredible, and because I didn't have a scholarship, Kevin and I had to support ourselves financially as well as paying for my studies. But Kevin couldn't work until he got a social security number and work permit, and that took several months to resolve. So I tried to hold down three part-time jobs so that we could stay afloat financially.

I have a real empathy with the thousands of students and families in South Africa who are trying to put their children through university, and quite honestly have no idea where the next cent is coming from. I have been there.

I worked as a graduate assistant in the International Office at the Harvard Graduate School of Education, and did odd jobs at the Alumni Office, as I had done while completing my Master's. In addition, I took on a few administrative tasks, but collectively, this wasn't nearly enough to keep us afloat. It was never going to be enough to pay for tuition and accommodation, let alone books and living expenses.

This period was both wonderful time and very tough: it really was 'the best of times, and the worst of times,' in the true Dickensian sense. By February 1994 we were in serious financial trouble, and the bitterly cold weather did nothing to lift our spirits.

As South Africans, we're accustomed to lots of sunshine, but Boston experienced one of its biggest snowstorms ever in February 1994: 19.4 inches of snow fell over two days that February.

And things had really been desperate. Four or five months after we arrived, our cupboards were so bare that we needed to make a drastic plan to get food. Kevin put his pride in his pocket and joined the snaking queue of folk at the Salvation Army to collect a food parcel so that we could have something to eat for the next few days.

When I had arrived at Harvard Housing, an American Express Gold credit card with $10 000 credit loaded onto it was waiting in the mailbox. Although it was very tempting, I never touched it. Coming from the Cape Flats, I knew that people who are poor and desperate to improve their lot or even just survive, can get into serious trouble when they use credit. I wasn't going to fall into that trap. As desperate as I was, I was determined not to use that credit card.

I tried to secure a loan from the local bank in Harvard Square, but this was declined. I tried to work harder, squeeze in more hours of part-time work. Stretched to my limits, I was still falling behind in my payments.

I truly know what it's like to hit rock bottom financially: I've experienced it first-hand. What made it even more difficult was having nothing, and living in a foreign country. I'd already double-bonded my small house in Cape Town. Kevin had tried to get casual work, but was unable to do so without a work visa. We were desperate.

Marriages can break down as a result of financial challenges. In your own circle of friends, no doubt you've heard stories of how relationships break down when one of the partners is either studying or studying and working. This happens very easily unless you find ways to have the difficult conversations. And Kevin and I had many of these kinds of conversations.

We agreed on how we were going to move our lives forward meaningfully, how we were going to work our way out of debt, how we were going to recover from taking all of this time out, how we would find a job, get back to a career, when we returned to South Africa.

Finally, his social security card arrived. Through a conversation he'd struck up with a man in the Salvation Army queue, Randy Brookes, he applied for a job as a packer at Sears, and got the job, earning $3 an hour for the next four months. He was so thrilled to have a job at last and be earning some money. When his first pay cheque arrived, he bought a mountain of groceries and bottle of $1.99 Chilean wine to celebrate with Randy and me.

Despite the extra income, however, we still weren't breaking even. Kevin studied for the American Council on Exercise exam, and passed. He was now certified to work in a gym as a floor instructor at $4 an hour.

He worked very long hours. He opened the gym at 5am and locked up at 10pm. He left home each morning on his bicycle at 4.30am, in the dark, and got back home at around 10.30pm – in the dark again.

Our very good friend, Edith Vries, who was also studying at Harvard at the time, kindly waited up for Kevin each night. As the elevator rose to the 22nd floor, it seemed as if it automatically stopped on the 15th floor so he could visit Edith. She always had a stiff whisky or a healthy portion of Cape Malay curry waiting for him on those sub-zero Boston nights. A network of South African friends and family played a hugely supportive role in our lives.

Kevin accepted any extra available work offered beyond the stipulated maximum of forty hours a week, and he did this seven days a week for the next three years. It didn't take him long to qualify as a personal trainer earning more than $10 an hour. Financially, things were beginning to look up.

Then I persuaded him to do a Master's in Human Movement at Boston University, but of course, that meant finding more money. So Kevin returned to South Africa to sell off all of his assets – a car, a motorcycle, a trailer. He even sold his most prized possessions: disco speakers he'd built himself, an amplifier, turntables and LPs. They represented decades of collection and hard work. But their sale meant he had R20 000 in his pocket, and he could start his studies. Every asset that he had accumulated over three decades of hard work was sold in one week, but at least now he had the money he needed.

The biggest challenge now, was how he would manage to balance his work and his studies. Finding time to do his lecture readings, research readings and study as well as hand in projects on time proved to be very draining. It was a very difficult period for both of us.

But it was also a period of great learning. Because it taught me the importance of humility. Irrespective of who you are and what you've achieved, you should never lose sight of this, and never be too proud to ask for help or share the difficulties that you are experiencing. Yours isn't the first hard-luck story that people have heard, and it certainly won't be the last.

We still weren't managing to cover our monthly expenses, even with the extra income. So I swallowed my pride, and with much trepidation, I decided to discuss the dilemma Kevin and I found ourselves in with Student Financial Aid at Harvard. I remember saying: "I've slipped behind with my payments. I haven't paid my tuition for some time. I haven't paid my accommodation for some time. I don't think I can continue. I think we'll have to go home."

Everything happened in slow motion. The woman from the Financial Aid Office got up very slowly, walked to the filing cabinet and pulled out my file. She looked at my payments and my performance to date and said: "If you continue performing like this we'll support you. We're going to pay your tuition fees and we're going to give you three teaching fellowships.

"You are privileged to work with these great professors. You should be able to survive on this, and also square up your debt. The only challenge is that you have to continue to perform at this level. We'll call you in six months' time and we'll have this conversation again."

I was in tears. Excited beyond belief, I very quickly learned what 'pay for performance' was all about. Every few months I had to account for my performance, to ensure that I did not lose heart and just opt to go home.

I knew I had to work as hard as possible to make this happen. I didn't have the luxury of completing a doctorate over a six- or seven-year period, as many of the other students did. I had to complete my doctorate as quickly as possible.

Having three supervisors proved very challenging. One would tell me to do something; the others disagreed. I, on the other hand, often wanted to do something completely different. I had to constantly triangulate to ensure that I kept going in the right direction.

I worked very hard and seldom knew the difference between night and day. At times there were blizzards and people were told not to venture out unless it was absolutely necessary, but this never stopped me from visiting the library.

There were a number of hurdles to overcome to complete the doctorate. There was the course work, which included statistics and quantitative methodology. Anyone who has tackled these subjects knows that they're very difficult. The second hurdle was to write a qualifying paper. This was reviewed by a panel of professors on the Committee for Higher Degrees. The third was the dissertation proposal. Only once this has been approved, could one start writing the dissertation.

But there was another, more important hurdle – Kevin's health. From very long hours of work and virtually no rest he had become very ill, with pins and needles in his hands and feet every night that were keeping him awake. The doctors couldn't tell him what was wrong, and he began to look haggard and lose weight as a result of the lack of sleep.

Finally an elderly doctor sat him down and chatted to Kevin about life in general. He prescribed two things: sunshine and rest. He recommended that we get away to somewhere warm for a week and just rest. What Kevin needed was Vitamin D from the sunshine, some laughter, fun and some very good rest. This all sounded awfully good to Kevin, but he was concerned that he could not afford such a trip, and he couldn't miss a week's salary.

So we began to save – and quickly – so that we could go on holiday. We'd seen a special advertised in the *Boston Globe* – an all-inclusive seven-night package to the romantic Caribbean island of Aruba for just $499. In September 1994 we were on our way. Within a day, Kevin's pins and needles had disappeared, his appetite had returned, and so had his libido – which was just as well, as my biological clock had started ticking. Loudly. Unbeknown to me, our son had been conceived during that week – which wasn't quite part of the plan. I never imagined that I'd conceive as quickly as I did.

But if I've learnt anything, it's that we can't live our lives in neat little boxes; we can't sequence and order things as rigidly as we might like to. Things have a way of just happening. We have to be receptive to what emerges. You have to be aware of this in terms of the way that you design your life, and the way in which you organise your milestones, your goals and your aspirations. As much as I'd have liked to have been ordered and sequenced and scientific about this, it didn't work out that way. And if you asked me to do it again, I wouldn't do it any differently.

My pregnancy was fuss-free. I remember slipping on the ice once or twice, but I was fine. I even returned to South Africa when I was four months pregnant to be my sister's bridesmaid.

When I returned to Boston, I continued to work night and day. I was surrounded by books. I wrote, thought, and rewrote. I cooked, visited the gynaecologist, worked at the university, and marked papers for the professors. I'd be up at six in the morning, work, sleep for two or three hours and then begin working again. When I submitted my qualifying paper in April 1995, I'd already written my dissertation proposal. I lived with a lot of faith and optimism that this would be approved, and that I would be able to get through the next hurdle.

Heavily pregnant at the time, I remember sitting nervously outside the door, with very sweaty palms, waiting for the committee to post the results, so that I could submit my dissertation proposal before giving birth. If I failed the qualifying paper, this would be the end of it. But they approved it with distinction, and my proposal was on track.

The experience taught me that if you have a sense of purpose, direction, a focus, you can do what you have to do in order to get things done. Despite the complexity of deadlines, we managed, somehow. But you can't do it on your own: you need to be surrounded by people who are very supportive, who care, and who take time out for you.

Chapter 7

Jamie is born

When Jamie was born, I was literally in the middle of my doctorate. I was still very active a week before Jamie's birth, and Kevin used to say: "This child won't know the difference between day and night because your sleeping patterns aren't normal day and night patterns."

I'd always had a fairly clinical view that I'd give birth, and that it would all be very simple. I chose to have a natural birth, and when I was admitted to Brigham and Women's Hospital in Boston at 4am on 23 May 1995, my contractions were one minute apart, and I thought it would all be over very soon. However, I only gave birth the following morning after almost twenty hours of labour and an episiotomy, at 1.13am.

Jamie was a very healthy, strong little boy. He weighed 3.7kg and was twenty inches long. They put him onto my chest, and he latched on and fed straight away. Two-and-a-half years later I was still struggling to get him off the breast.

It's difficult to put into words what it felt like to set eyes on him and hold him for the very first time – every mother knows what I'm talking about. Kevin was by my side for the entire labour, and Jamie's birth was a very emotional experience for both of us.

My sister-in-law, Denise Zinn, and my friend, Edith Vries, were with me throughout my labour. Denise is married to Kevin's brother, Allan, and she and I were completing our doctorates at Harvard at the same time. Denise and Edith literally held my legs up and I pushed my feet into their ribs, wanting the relief of the baby being born.

Cell phones weren't as evolved as they are today, so we made good use of landlines to keep the family informed. We had provided our families with telephonic updates regularly throughout my pregnancy, and throughout the labour there were several calls to report progress. My mother kept saying: "I wish I could be there." It would've been wonderful to have her at Jamie's birth, but unfortunately none of us were in a position to pay for her air ticket.

We called our family in South Africa immediately after Jamie was born. Kevin's mother, Jean, said: "I thought it would be a really tiny baby, and that I would have difficulty even holding the baby. When I saw how big he was, I would've been able to cope with him." She too, would've loved to have been at Jamie's birth. She kept saying: "I should've come over. I should've saved more." But I reassured everyone that we'd be home very soon.

We named Jamie after my dad and Kevin's dad. My father is James, and Kevin's dad is Reuben, so we named him Jamie, a diminutive of James, and gave him the middle name of Reuben.

Twenty-four hours after Jamie's arrival, we were discharged, and Jamie had already been issued with his American birth certificate.

It was a fairly hot day – around 34°C. I love the Charles River, so I dressed Jamie, put him in his pram, and walked along the river banks. Perhaps 'hobbled' is a better description – walking was painful, as I was full of stitches. While I was out, I ran into a colleague's mother, who was visiting at the time: "Is this the new baby you gave birth to only yesterday?" she asked. "Please go home right this minute! You shouldn't be out here with him at all."

It could have been a very different experience navigating the first few months of our baby's life in a foreign country. But Kevin, Jamie and I were shown so much love and we were showered with gifts. As a result, we never felt alone or isolated, despite the fact that our families and support systems were so far away.

I returned to work at the International Office as soon as I possibly could, and I carried Jamie with me wherever I went. Rosalind Micahelles, who was responsible for the International Office, very kindly allowed me to bring Jamie to work. Everyone was very welcoming, and Jamie slept while I worked in the office.

The plan was to have the dissertation proposal approved and to return to Cape Town to write the dissertation, and this is what we did, returning to South Africa two months later.

I wrote my dissertation for my doctorate at home, the topic being "Anti-Racist Education Teacher Perspectives." Email wasn't as robust as it is now, so I relied heavily on Federal Express and DHL. I would send off a version, and eagerly wait for feedback.

Harvard's support and faith in me paid off; I graduated with a Doctorate in Education in June 1997.

After I'd completed my doctorate, it was very tempting to stay in the US and work there, but, I wanted to return to South Africa so that I could make a difference in our new democracy. Kevin and I were in Boston when South Africa held its first democratic elections in 1994. Excited, and very proud to be able to vote for the very first time in our lives, we voted at the Boston City Hall. Acknowledging the historical significance of the day, the Kennedy School of Government threw a celebratory party and many South Africans attended.

I attribute much of my success to the wonderful people who surrounded me at Harvard, all of whom have contributed enormously to thought leadership in education, and all of whom are still my friends. I learnt so much from every one of them. I'm a better academic, and a better person because of their influence.

Professor Claryce Evans was my primary supervisor for my doctorate, and I am still in touch with her. Professor Vito Perrone was also one of my supervisors, and I was a teaching fellow on his teaching and learning programme. He was a genius at what education really means. Sadly, he has since passed away. Professor Bruce Fuller was my third supervisor.

And then there was Professor Eleanor Duckworth. I was a teaching fellow for her famous T-440 class, which focuses on how children learn, and discovering innovative ways of teaching. She views learning as developing understanding, and teaching as helping learners to construct their own understanding.

I attended her retirement event in May 2013 at Harvard. I also wrote a piece that was published in a book presented to Eleanor, on her retirement. Eleanor taught us how to think for ourselves and taught us about learning how to learn. This translates into "making something out of what we have". Through her teachings we learned how make meaning through thinking and not simply being given the answer. I loved the theme of making something out of what we have. It resonated with me as I felt that was exactly what I had been trying to do all my life.

As a South African, I've been inspired by Eleanor's words and have taken strength from them. Eleanor enabled and empowered us as students to think deeply and critically, to have the courage to challenge and question, to drive change in education, and more broadly in society, so that we might indeed make a difference in this world.

Eleanor has been a relentless champion for integrated schools, as opposed to racial and class-based education, and has been an activist for "education for all" and progressive education. She has also been a tireless crusader for social justice, women's rights, peace, educational development and fighting poverty. She has left an indelible impact on my life and way of being, and has influenced countless others through her work to turn the tide on education.

I believe that empowerment comes from something Eleanor is passionate about: emancipatory education, where we are able to become activists for an education that makes a lasting, meaningful impact on society and the lives of children through courageous conversations, discovery and exploration, adventure, and dance.

The experience of learning from Eleanor's teaching enabled us, as her students, to take teaching and learning to a new level and generate a new passion for learning. Her philosophy is that children want to make sense of the world and don't simply want to have the 'answer', as this limits and stops their thinking.

I recall sessions on the meaning of 'messing about' – play and fun as a way to make deeper meaning of perplexing concepts. We were encouraged to try out new thinking without feeling dumb. But sadly, too many hours at school are still spent on memorisation and tests that have nothing to do with real learning, inventiveness and curiosity.

Eleanor teaches us that "real learning, attentive real learning, deep learning is playful, frustrating and joyful and discouraging, so exciting, sociable and private all the time, which is what makes it great".(Duckworth, Faculty Speech, May 23, 2012) She also teaches us that "teaching is helping people to learn, and you have not taught if people have not learned". (Duckworth, February 15, 2012) These are powerful insights that every educator needs to reflect on if they are to teach with lasting impact. My wish is that we take our learnings and make a radical difference in education across the world and in South Africa.

Education has the potential to liberate one; education has certainly liberated me from poverty. I'd like to encourage all teachers and leaders in South Africa to inspire young people to push beyond their boundaries, and to support them as they do so. Teachers play a critical role in learners' lives: their influence should never be underestimated.

There are many challenges in the South African education system, many of them linked to our history of apartheid-based education. There is much to be done to ensure an effective turnaround in South African education so that all children have access to quality education that will enable them to grow and thrive.

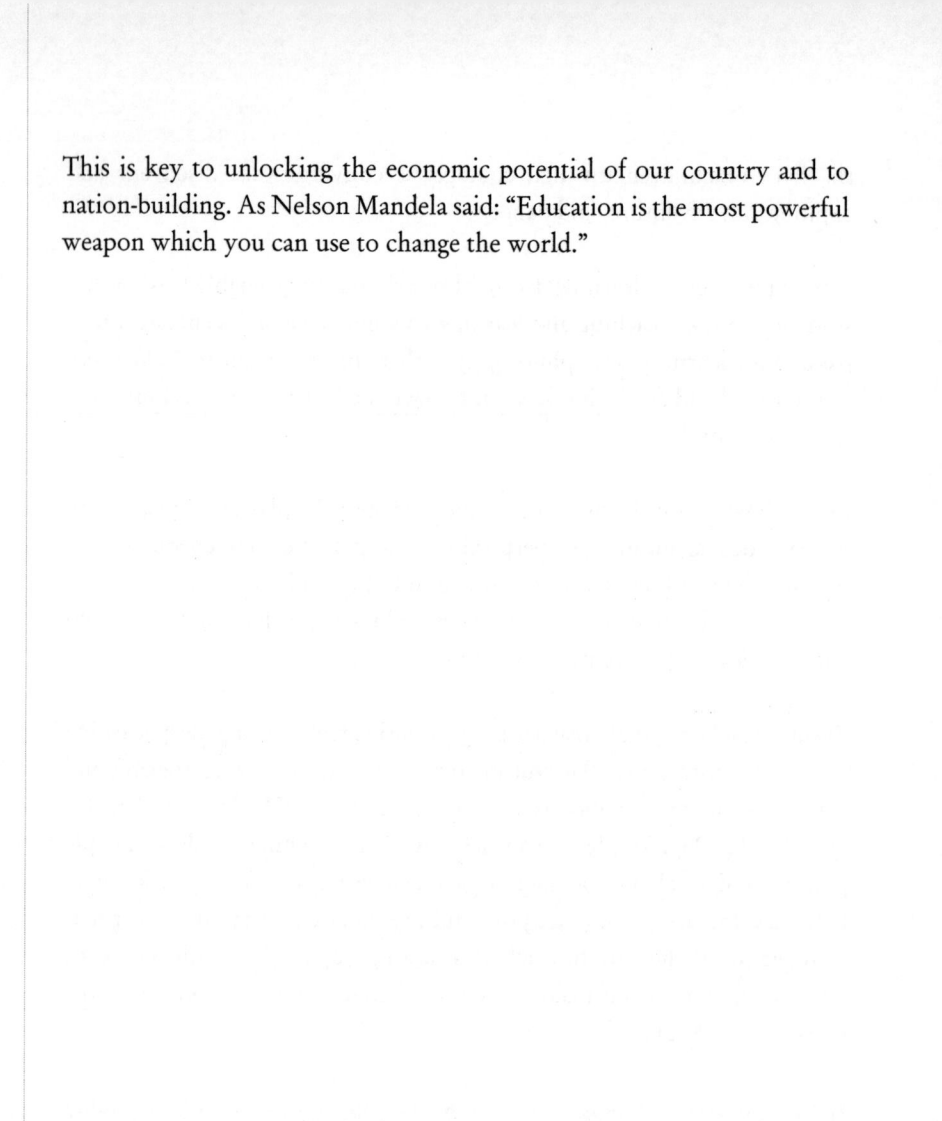

This is key to unlocking the economic potential of our country and to nation-building. As Nelson Mandela said: "Education is the most powerful weapon which you can use to change the world."

Chapter 8

Returning to South Africa

When we returned to South Africa so that I could write my Doctoral thesis, we walked out into the arrivals hall to a welcoming party of note at Cape Town International Airport. I couldn't believe the number of people who were there to meet us. Everyone was very curious to see Jamie, who was already three months old.

Both sets of proud grandparents couldn't wait to see their grandchild and hold him for the first time. He was the first grandchild on my side of the family and the third grandchild on Kevin's side. Jamie was a beautiful child and everyone fell in love with him the instant they set eyes on him.

Our decision to return to South Africa was a conscious one: Kevin and I wanted to bring Jamie home to South Africa, so that he could be with his family. Kevin and I were also determined to make a difference in the new South Africa that was unfolding.

We were thrilled to be back in the midst of our family and friends, but it wasn't an easy time for us as Kevin struggled to find employment.

I returned to the UWC at the end of my maternity leave. It was a very busy time: I was working, writing a thesis, breastfeeding and doing all of the wonderful things associated with being a mother. I'm the first to acknowledge that this wouldn't have been possible without the support of Kevin and my wonderful extended family. Once again, everyone rose to the occasion, to provide me with a loving, supportive environment.

I submitted the final version of my Doctoral thesis to Harvard towards the end of 1996 after almost ten years in academia.

When I returned to the UWC my head had already moved on: it was time for me to tackle new challenges, to assume a new role, if I was to make a difference. I wanted to make a difference in more pragmatic ways, and I'd set my heart on working for the Department of Education in the Western Cape.

I had a burning passion for education, and I wanted to use the knowledge that I'd gained at Harvard while completing my doctorate, to help to create a better education system and better education policies, even if this was initially only at a provincial level.

But life sometimes deals us an unexpected hand: they aren't always the cards you'd choose. I applied for a number of jobs at the Department of Education in the Western Cape, including curriculum development positions, administrative, and middle management positions. I went for two job interviews, but I was told that my profile didn't match any of the positions on offer.

One of the things that I've learnt is that you have to pick yourself up when things don't go your way. You have to dust yourself off and commit to doing even greater things. At times like these you need to make a conscious decision to be resilient and to swim upstream, if that's what it's going to take. I firmly believe that setbacks and adversity lead to resilience. Resilience, essentially, is the ability to bounce back when life throws you a curve-ball. And as I was to learn, there would be a few more curve-balls to come.

On 14 April 1997 I was in my office at Southern Life when the phone rang. The call was from Harvard. The person at the other end of the line asked me to provide them with a fax number so that they could fax me a letter with the outcome of the committee's deliberation on my doctoral thesis. I had to wait for the fax to know the final outcome of all those years of hard work.

I sweated beads of blood waiting for the fax to come through – it seemed to take ages! Finally, the machine sprang to life, and, excited and nervous at the same time, I anxiously grabbed the fax with both hands; the page was still warm. My doctoral thesis had been approved, and a graduation date had been set: I was to graduate on 6 June, which also happens to be Kevin's birthday.

I went crazy. I remember running up and down the passage with the fax in my hand. The next person in my doctoral programme cohort finished a year after me. The remainder of the class finished in their six or seventh year.

Kevin and I booked our air tickets and made plans to attend my graduation. I was very disappointed that we couldn't afford to fly my mom and dad to Boston with us. They'd provided me with so much emotional support during this period, and they'd also instilled the seed in me that education would liberate me and uplift my family out of poverty.

But I have some truly wonderful friends in Boston, and this includes Steve Schultz who is also Jamie's god-father. When Steve heard that I was graduating, he said my parents had to attend the graduation. Knowing that Kevin and I were cash-strapped, he generously paid for my parents' air tickets, and insisted that we stay with him.

My graduation at Harvard was one of the greatest moments in my life. It was an awesome experience, and one I'll never forget. I was very emotional at my graduation, because of all that I'd gone through. I was completely overwhelmed.

We had to do an oral presentation. I remember standing up in front of all of those people. And I remember Jamie, who had just turned two years old, and who was a very active toddler, running up and down the aisles while my mother tried to calm him down.

*****

Despite the initial disappointment of the door closing very firmly to a career with the Department of Education in the Western Cape, other doors opened. I've learnt that one needs to be pragmatic; dreams are often realised in a different shape and in a different place. As the great Nelson Mandela put it: "The greatest glory in living lies not in never falling, but in rising every time we fall."

Which is how I'd come to be at Southern Life. Sitting at my mother's house, paging through a copy of the *Cape Times* one day, I'd seen that Southern Life in Newlands was looking for a training manager. Although I'd never worked in a corporate environment, as I scrutinised the job specifications, I realised I could do most of the tasks that the position required. Kevin dropped off my application while at cycling training, and I kept my fingers crossed. It was truly a shot in the dark.

I was invited for an interview two weeks later. They weren't too keen on all my academic qualifications, and felt that because I hadn't worked in a corporate environment before, there were risks in considering me for the role. The HR director said: "You haven't worked at a corporate before. Why are you applying for this position? With all of these qualifications, you should stay on at the university." I explained that I wanted to do something different from pure academia. I wanted to apply everything that I'd learnt in a different and innovative way, in a different space.

Southern Life decided to take a chance with me. They asked me whether I was prepared to take a risk. I replied: "Yes, what is the risk?" I'd leave everything that I'd known for the past ten years and work for Southern Life on a six-month probation period. Both parties had a twenty-four hour notice period.

I discussed the job offer with Kevin, and we agreed that progressing in your career always entails risks and taking on new challenges. There are times when you have to take calculated risks and throw caution to the wind, even if you know it's not going to be easy. I knew I had to take risks if I were to make progress. I had to get out of my comfort zone and not allow the fear of the unknown to distract me.

There are many things that come our way that we have to do for the first time. I also learned that most people "wing it" through these first-time events, and do so successfully because they believe in themselves. They don't say, "I can't do it because I have never done it before." They just do it. Fear of failure when taking on new things is quite natural. I know I keep quoting Nelson Mandela, but he just puts things so well: "It seems impossible until it's done." Being optimistic and remaining positive are critical to success.

I accepted the job offer, and felt the adrenaline coursing through my body. Had I made the right decision? Would this decision come back and bite me one day? My colleagues at UWC were very disappointed to see me leave, and they did everything to convince me to stay, but my mind was made up. I started at Southern Life in April 1997 and my mother retired from Reader's Digest to look after Jamie.

I loved working at Great Westerford on the leafy Newlands Main Road. Southern Life was a well-respected company that had been around for decades. I wanted to learn as much as possible, and true to form, do so as quickly as possible.

I'd previously believed completing a doctorate at Harvard was the hardest thing I had ever done: I was mistaken. My capabilities were tested and the learning curve that lay before me proved to be very steep. As the training manager, I had to identify training needs, source the training and, in some instances, even design and facilitate the training. I sat down with line managers and assessed their training needs.

Whereas I'd previously lived in the academic delivery space, I was now living through the entire education value chain. I was addressing questions such as: "What does learning mean in an organisation? What sort of learning is required?"

A few months into my time at Southern Life, the First Rand Group made a pitch for Southern Life. There were some retrenchments and the remainder of Southern Life was sucked into Momentum Life, to form the MMI Group.

Some Southern Life staff took the opportunity offered to move to Centurion, in Pretoria; others took the retrenchment package that was offered. While this was my first experience of retrenchment, it certainly wouldn't be my last. Although I remained at Southern Life to almost the end, uncertain about what might happen to my own position, I decided to apply for other roles.

While at Southern Life, I established very good relationships with the First Rand Group and with the people at Momentum. I've learnt that it's very important to build very good relationships with people. From my own experience I've also learnt that it's possible for people who've completed a doctorate or post-doctoral programme to fill other roles, to do things other than being an academic. I hope that my life's journey will enable students in an academic environment to view life through a different lens, to see that they're able to make a much wider contribution.

Chapter 9

Life often has other ideas

There are times in your life when you fly by the seat of your pants. There are also times when you have to wing it. However, neither are my preferred options, even if life often has other ideas.

I applied for a position at what was then called the South African Management Development Institute (SAMDI) in January 1998. The Department of Public Service and Administration, to which SAMDI reported, invited me for a job interview in May of that year.

Since I'd applied for the position many months previously and had applied for a few roles, I couldn't recall what position I had applied for, and was too embarrassed to ask. To make matters worse, I couldn't find the advertisement for this specific role, so I had to pick up cues during the interview.

I was very nervous, but I flew to Johannesburg, and took a taxi from the airport to SAMDI's offices in Pretoria. I was stressed: not knowing the exact position I was applying for meant that I couldn't really prepare for the interview.

Luckily, the panel that was going to interview me was running late, which was a real blessing in disguise. While sitting in reception, I paged through some of the government publications. I read about transformation, the new regulations, the new leadership and the new operating model. When the interview started, the questions I was asked were related to everything that I'd read during the previous half an hour.

And so, I was offered the role of Director: Special Programmes at SAMDI in Pretoria, which meant we would have to move. The thought of moving to Pretoria is inconceivable for most Capetonians: most of us believe that lifestyle outweighs opportunity. Kevin had recently accepted a job offer in Cape Town, so I flew back knowing that I would have to ask him how he felt about relocating to Pretoria. I would be led by the look on his face when I broached the subject. He'd already followed me halfway around the world once before, so I knew this was a big ask. I'd only accept the job offer if he was in total agreement.

Kevin being Kevin, he said: "Let's do this," and put my career first. He graciously gave up his job and moved the family to Pretoria. We asked Kevin's parents whether they'd like to move with us. Jean and Reuben did the most unbelievable thing: they told us they'd love to do so, and would help us look after Jamie. They sold their house in Cape Town and we all made the trek up North together.

We moved to Pretoria in August 1998. This was supposed to be a three-year plan. Seventeen years later, we were still living in Gauteng. Life doesn't always work out the way you expect it to.

Despite having a Master's in Human Movement and many years of experience in both education and sport, Kevin struggled to find a job in Pretoria. But he never allows it to get him down, and always comes up with some way to ensure he's productive and employed.

Kevin found a man selling firewood on a street corner. The man told Kevin where to buy wood for R10 and sell it for R30, so there was a period where Kevin kept busy and also contributed to the family coffers by selling wood and firelighters. I'm very proud of him for doing this.

Meanwhile, my work at SAMDI involved strategic advising, consulting, researching, designing, facilitating and co-ordinating national and provincial training programmes for public service managers. It also involved translating new public service regulations and policy into training programmes for public service managers, with a view to facilitating and accelerating implementation.

The key objective of the training was to drive the overall change and transformation of the public service. I enjoyed the work and met many fascinating people during this interesting phase of South Africa's journey as a fledgling democracy.

Another interesting development on the academic front came in December 1999, when I received a letter from the University of Pretoria's Faculty of Economics and Management Sciences inviting me to become an Extraordinary Professor. I was not expecting this and was elated at this recognition.

An Extraordinary Professor meant that I was not full-time but would be requested from time to time to present at special lectures, serve on the Faculty Advisory Board, and generally advise and support the work of the university. I continue to hold this position, which has given me the opportunity to work with and learn from the most amazing academics and experts in the field of Economics and Management Sciences.

My next job after SAMDI would be in a very different sector: IT. I was introduced to the MD of Infracom by Andries van Zyl, who thought that my value would be better placed in a corporate. I was invited me to apply for the role of HR Director, and a few months later, Infracom was integrated into a listed IT company, Computer Configurations Holdings (CCH).

I was not appointed to the position of Human Resource Director at CCH, but to the newly created position of Group Executive for Employment Equity. This was an exciting role, required by the Employment Equity Act, 1998, to drive employment equity and rectify apartheid inequalities in the workplace. I was thrilled to be appointed to a position where I could make a difference and help to address the injustices of our country's past. I worked very closely with CCH CEO, Aletha Ling. CCH was the only IT company as I recall that was led by a woman. Aletha proved a wonderful role model and I learnt a great deal from her.

Aletha has pursued a very successful career in the IT industry for the past 30 years. She has a wealth of experience and insight into technology, sales, marketing, and general management. Aletha taught me that having a broad and deep understanding of business is a prerequisite for success.

Although I'd learnt very early in my career that continuous learning is vital for success in any endeavour, working in the fast-paced and ever-changing IT environment reinforced just how important it is to be fully committed to continuous learning, irrespective of your role within the organisation. I really admire Aletha for being a serial innovator, founding, nurturing and selling a number of ventures in various industries such as healthcare, financial services and presentation services.

Aletha has left an indelible imprint on my life. The qualities that have resonated with me and remained with me throughout my career, would be her passion for radical innovation, her tenacity through tough assignments, and her ability to lead in difficult times. These qualities make a huge difference in every area of business.

Most importantly, she taught me the importance of being a good listener, being sincere and being authentic. I really admire the fact that Aletha always challenges conventional wisdom and pushes our thinking to new levels. We need leaders who can inspire us to do more than we believe is possible; we need to become such leaders.

So there I was, working with this amazing woman. I wasn't in the job market, and I certainly wasn't looking when Zane Reddiar, a young, relentless and very enterprising head-hunter, approached me out of the blue. He told me that Reckitt Benckiser, the world's number one in household cleaning goods, listed on the London Stock Exchange, and a well-respected company in the global fast moving consumer goods (FMCG) industry, was looking for a regional director of human resources for Africa Middle East (AME). The company had just gone through a global merger: Reckitt and Colman merged with Benckiser and huge culture shifts were needed to ensure a seamless transition.

Despite Zane's protests, I refused to look at the proposal that he'd put forward for my consideration. I was adamant that I had no intention of leaving CCH. After much nagging on Zane's part, I eventually relented, and opened the envelope that he'd left on my desk. It was mid-December. I wanted to see why he was so persistent that I should at least look at the offer. I took the offer home. Kevin and I always make important decisions together. After one of our clarification conversations, we agreed that this option was worth exploring.

I rang Zane the next morning and told him that I was prepared to meet with AME Senior Vice President, Mike Waddington. It was a huge step up from my current position at CCH. I knew that Aletha would understand if I got the position, as this was a global opportunity.

My meeting with Mike went very well. I left the meeting very excited, even exhilarated, at the prospect of possibly working in Africa and the Middle East. I knew this experience would broaden my career horizons significantly; it would also add much needed international experience to my CV.

I was invited to fly to London to meet the executive vice-president for HR and a few other senior executives. The meeting in London was uplifting. I returned to South Africa hoping to be offered the position, and my appointment was confirmed a week later. I dreaded breaking the news to Aletha, but she recognised that I'd been offered a wonderful opportunity to build my career and grow as an individual, so I left CCH with her blessing. I started in my new position in January 2001.

I thoroughly enjoyed my time at Reckitt Benckiser. I particularly enjoyed the fact that I worked with a very diverse team comprising Italian, German, Indian, African and British colleagues. I firmly believe that diversity and inclusion are enriching, foster creativity, and provide companies with a competitive edge. I travelled extensively into Africa and the Middle East during this period, which provided me with new perspectives and broadened my world-view.

Travel kept me from home for longer than I had anticipated, and when the regional office was moved from Johannesburg to Dubai, life became even more of a balancing act. I empathise with women who find themselves in this position. Even with the best support system in place, one is still torn between work, children and family responsibilities, and the possible burn-out from trying to do it all perfectly.

Jamie was growing up very fast, and his granny, Jean, helped Kevin and me enormously by co-ordinating all of his extramural activities. At seven years of age, Jamie had grown into a physically strong and determined child, who enjoyed sport – much like his dad and both grandfathers.

During my time at Reckitt Benckiser I made very sure that I spent as much time as I could with Jamie and Kevin, despite my hectic travel schedule. It's amazing how that awareness of being away from my loved ones made the times when we were together even more important and purposeful.

I've always believed that it's the quality of time, not the quantity of time spent together that's important. Don't be an hour counter and then try to apportion measures of guilt to yourself. Life and giving of yourself is about more than hours in the day.

It's the reason our annual holiday meant so much to us. It was something we looked forward to as a family: a time to catch up with friends and family, and to spend quality time together. We were relaxed and happy as we headed for Mossel Bay that January, filled up with the love of our families.

So there we were, driving along Jan Smuts after a wonderful festive season. We turned onto the N2, we passed the airport and I was changing a CD because Jamie didn't like the song. I remember him complaining about his seatbelt. I remember passing the airport. And then I don't remember anything.

At Mew Way near Khayelitsha, just after 1pm on 3 January 2003, a young man struck us at speed from behind. The impact was so great that it uncoupled the caravan from our double-cab bakkie causing both the caravan and bakkie to roll a few times. The young driver broke his collar bone and his car only came to a standstill about fifty metres away from the crash site.

I don't recall the impact at all. I remember nothing except the seatbelt and the CD and the airport. But for twenty-four hours at Vincent Palloti Hospital, no-one knew whether or not I would make it.

It was one of those horrific car accidents you hear about. Jamie fell out of the car when it rolled. I was unconscious and trapped inside the vehicle. I have no idea how Kevin managed to get out of the overturned vehicle and pull me out. It was a Friday afternoon, a clear, sunny day. If I had been leaning over the seat to help Jamie, my injuries would have been far, far worse.

The newspaper carried the story the next day. There was a photograph of the paramedics working on Jamie, trying to save him, but they couldn't, despite their very best efforts. I am very grateful to all the paramedics who helped at the scene.

My only son, my beautiful boy who loved life so much, died at the scene of the accident, and I didn't know it had happened, because I was fighting for my own life. I remember waking up in hospital not knowing where I was, and trying to understand what was going on. I couldn't see a thing. My head was badly injured and my face was bruised and swollen. My heart was broken.

There was a lot of activity around me in the hospital; doctors and nurses were trying to save me. I knew something terrible had happened, but I couldn't comprehend what. I recall someone calmly telling me that I'd been in an MVA [motor vehicle accident]. I had no idea what that meant.

Being unable to move or see, I had to rely on what I could hear, and on what people told me. As I listened to the subdued conversations around me, I made the connection. A woman told me I was badly injured, and that she was going to 'clean me up'. Her voice was quite loud and close to my face. I assume she thought I couldn't hear her very well.

When I asked her where Jamie and Kevin were, the nurse said they were being transported by helicopter to the hospital: "They're coming. They're still at the scene. They're bringing them. They're okay. Don't worry."

Confused and terrified, I couldn't piece together what had happened, so I decided to wait, and listen for the sounds of a helicopter, but I could hear nothing other than hushed whispers and beeping machines.

I'm not sure how much time passed before I heard Kevin's voice and my mother's voice. Even though I couldn't see them, I was relieved to have them finally standing beside me, holding me. Kevin, battling back his tears, hesitantly, and very gently, told me that Jamie had passed away. The paramedics had done everything they possibly could to save him, but his injuries were too severe.

I couldn't believe what I was hearing. I tried telling myself that it was only a nightmare, that I'd wake up and everything would be as before. Unfortunately, the nightmare wasn't just a bad dream; we were living the nightmare and we had to deal with it.

I can only imagine how much courage it must have taken for Kevin, Mom, Dad and Merle to break this terrible news to me. When they told me the story later, they explained that they'd debated whether it was going to be a good thing to tell me now. What if something happened to me and they hadn't told me? What would be the best thing to do? They felt it would be better to just tell me.

The accident left me with serious head injuries, two fractured vertebrae, a broken arm, and a shifted patella. For twenty-four hours it was touch and go. They weren't sure I was going to make it. Part of me still believes that I left this world with my son and later came back. Regardless of what happened on that day, I realised how fine the line is between life and death – even for those of us who'd like to believe we are invincible.

Kevin had not escaped unscathed. Apart from fractured ribs he also had many cuts and bruises. But the physical aches and pains and injuries were nothing compared to the emotional anguish. We were heartbroken and devastated.

In just a few seconds our lives had changed completely, irrevocably. Our beautiful, healthy son had passed away at the tender age of seven: a harsh reality we struggled to accept. Once the news broke, my ward quickly filled with concerned and mourning family members and friend, who held us with their love, support and care.

My family never thought I was going to make it. They never thought I'd survive the first twenty-four hours, let alone live my life and pick myself up from the emotional devastation.

I couldn't do anything – my sister said my head looked like a large, battered and bruised pumpkin, and I had severe damage to my back that took long-term physiotherapy to ensure I became mobile again. So I had to lie still in my hospital bed while Kevin attended to everything. He bravely bore the heart-breaking task of making the funeral arrangements all by himself, while maintaining a constant vigil at my bedside.

We laid Jamie to rest on 11 January 2003. I was discharged from hospital in time to pay my last respects to our son, in a church packed to capacity. I don't know where all those attending the funeral came from, because most people were on holiday and were just returning home, but they came to support us. It was a great commemoration of Jamie's short life and a huge support for us, which helped to carry us through this dreadful period.

I'll always be very grateful for the way Kevin navigated me through the trauma of losing Jamie. I don't even know all of the things that Kevin had to do in the background, because I was incapable of doing anything to assist him at the time. Despite the horror of our situation, Kevin never fell apart; he was very strong, supportive and focused throughout the process, although of course Jamie's death affected him very deeply. But Kevin always reminds me that the day he lost his beloved son, he lost his soul; he exists only in person.

Kevin was so attached to and loved Jamie so dearly that today still, thirteen years after the tragedy, he finds great difficulty in just being reminded about it. He knelt by Jamie's side and saw the life drain from him. There was nothing that he could do to save his son's life and those memories haunt him daily.

A passer-by, Carlyn van der Schyff, who was first on the scene of the accident, held Jamie's hand with Kevin until the very last. We will always treasure Carlyn for being there. I later discovered that I had taught Carlyn at Groenvlei Secondary School and I had not seen her since she was a teenager. She is now a medical doctor.

They say that time heals, but after all this time, even as I write this story, I still cannot adequately find the words to express my emotions.

And then, as I was putting this book together, my beautiful seventeen-year-old niece and soul-mate to Jamie, Erin, was diagnosed as having panic attacks in November 2014. She was bright, energetic, swam for Western Province, her passion for swimming inspired by Jamie. When the doctors finally decided to do a brain scan on 23 March 2015, during her matric year at Bergvliet High, they discovered she wasn't having panic attacks: she had a brain tumour. She passed away a few weeks later.

This was very traumatic for the entire family, more especially Merle and Mark. The horrific realisation to Ma and Pa Jeftha was that they had now lost their second and only remaining grandchild. I have no words to describe this pain. I have had to draw on everything I know, all the emotions and learnings about grief and loss I had with Jamie, to support my sister, her husband, and my parents through yet another wave of tragedy.

Chapter 10

Facing our personal Everest

Kevin and I both faced many months of physical and emotional recovery, but we also faced our personal Everest: trying to piece back our shattered lives. The first few months were incredibly tough and Kevin and I really struggled. Unless you've suffered the trauma of losing a child, you can only intellectualise the emotional trauma that you go through. The emotional pain is by far worse than any physical pain.

Healing, in my case, meant months of physiotherapy and mountains of medication. I never thought I was going to make it. Battered, bruised and totally depleted emotionally, I was in a deep abyss: I couldn't see how I'd be able to get on with my life. I'd been asked on many occasions to swim upstream; this time I was being asked to swim against a tidal wave.

Kevin and I went for counselling – something I knew, from all the theory I'd learnt over the years, was critical to our healing process. After two or three sessions, however, I realised I had to find my own way to pull myself through this. Counselling by itself wasn't going to get me where I needed to be. I needed to push my internal boundaries.

At a conscious level I knew that true healing could only come from within, and that I had to find a way forward somehow. I know now that it is impossible to make peace with a loss like this. You can't ever completely get over it but you can work through it. Kevin and I faced a daily battle dealing with our emotions.

You have to find an internal source of strength to see yourself through every single day. It becomes a day-to-day process of healing, of acknowledging that this terrible thing has happened. You have to constantly guard against living in denial, against hoping that he's going to come back somehow and you're going to be able to change things. Instead you have to accept that it has happened, that you're still there, and that there's some sort of purpose in what's happened.

It's very easy to slide into a sea of dark despair, to try and cope with life by swallowing as many pills as you possibly can, never finding the inner strength to lift yourself up. Ultimately, what it comes down to is your own inner dialogue to find that strength, and to draw on all the positive energy that everybody sends you at a time like this.

It's important to be able to feel your own pain. It's important to not try and ignore it, but to actually feel it, understand it, and confront it. It's important not to defer it and not to try to get around it, but to know that you are experiencing this agony and that there's a good reason why you're feeling the way that you do.

It's also okay to cry. Crying isn't a sign of weakness, and it isn't a sign that you've lost the plot. It's a sign that we're human; it's part of the healing. We must allow ourselves to cry, and we must also allow others around us to cry.

Sometimes people want to offer advice. They have the very best intentions, but this often backfires. I've often found myself wishing someone hadn't said what they'd said, but decided that it came from a good place. But it's taught me when you're dealing with other people's traumas, you have to tread very carefully, and to think through what you want to say before saying it. Always put yourself in the other person's shoes. Having said this, however, it's always good to listen to the voices of people who care for you; it's good sometimes to listen to dissenting voices.

I chose to return to Harvard as part of my healing process. Harvard is where I'd fallen pregnant; where I'd given birth to Jamie. The Harvard community had been so much part of our lives, and everyone we knew there had always showered Jamie with so much love.

People were genuinely concerned and deeply distressed about what had happened. They invited me into their homes, as they wanted to hear what had happened. They wanted to be there, to provide me with lots of love and support. I found it very therapeutic. We'd been through so much together, and because we had so many shared memories, we could cry together, and there were times when we could even laugh.

Spending a week at Harvard was like closing a loop. As painful as it was, I knew I had to go back to the hospital where Jamie was born. I had to walk the streets that we'd walked and meet the people we'd spent time with. I returned to South Africa with new resolve.

But even today, there are still triggers – the smell of popcorn in airports, the sight of a child running with flowers in his hands to welcome his mother home from a long overseas trip. Things like these can trigger an enormous surge of emotion.

Reckitt Benckiser was amazing during this time and I have to thank Salvatore Caizzone who was Head of Africa Middle East at the time for his empathy. The doctors had given me six months sick leave and the company granted me this leave without hesitation, proof that there are organisations that have a soul, and that genuinely care about their people. As ruthless as the company is about chasing numbers and achieving financial targets and increasing its revenues, they were equally keen to see me get better, become functional again. We need to create organisations that care, because people go through various levels of trauma every day.

Slowly, but surely, I started reading again and I also started going out – both signs of progress. It was important to try to face people and to leave the safe cocoon of home. After two months at home, I felt that I needed to go back and immerse myself in my work.

A few months after returning to work I was overseas on business. Lying alone in my hotel room in Dubai with a picture of Jamie in front of me, I remember thinking: "What am I doing here? I should be home with family and friends. Perhaps I should focus on something in South Africa." I had to acknowledge that this part of the job wasn't working for me anymore.

With hindsight, I recognise that I went back to work far too soon after the accident. My work at Reckitt Benckiser entailed a lot of travelling, and I just wasn't ready for that yet.

Since it was a lean, mean and achievement-driven organisation, I didn't believe that it was fair to the company if I stayed on, so I resigned, not knowing whether I'd ever recover emotionally or find a new role after my recovery.

I was totally preoccupied with trying to get physically better. I was also trying to grasp the full impact of what had happened, and trying to mend myself in the process. I was fighting an inner battle: "I can do this. I'm going to get myself going again."

I gave myself a few months' grace, in an effort to regroup and reground. I registered Shirley Zinn Consulting in 2003. I thought I'd stay at home and do a few small projects. I never thought I'd ever return to corporate life.

Taking time out for personal healing is very important, but it is something very few people do after a traumatic event. After a few months, the emotional fragility I felt began to wane, and I opted to take on small projects, as a way of testing myself and rebuilding my confidence.

Jamie is a key part of the story that I want to tell. When he was alive, he was crucial in defining my life. Since he has passed away, he still plays a vital role in determining what gives me purpose, helping me figure out what to focus on, and living a real life of meaning.

People say time heals and it becomes easier over time. There's an element of that, but the loss remains very real. And even though time has moved on, you find yourself thinking about where this child would be if he'd grown up, what he'd be like, what he'd be doing. While we smile at the memories, our hearts are still very sore at our loss.

People often ask: "What was Jamie like?" To Kevin and me, Jamie was the most beautiful child in the world. He was the centre of our entire universe.

Jamie was a very happy baby and grew into a very busy, very industrious little boy.

I used to look at his face at night as he slept and think: "He's almost angelic. I hope nothing ever happens to him, I hope he lives a great life. I don't know what I would do if anything ever happens to him." Those thoughts often return to haunt me.

Jamie loved being breastfed. His first words were: "Want some nana now, nana, nana, nana." Nana meant my breast. When I tried to wean Jamie, I tried to rationalise with him: "Jamie, you're too big [he was two-and-a-half years old by then]. You can't have this anymore." I wouldn't do this differently if I had to do it all over again – we each have to find the best way for our own children.

Jamie loved things with wheels that he could move around and play with, so his first birthday cake was a train. He was also a real water baby. Kevin taught him to swim before he could even walk, and our gym in Constantia gave us a special dispensation to allow him to use the pool.

He even managed to get me to swim during winter. Year round, he'd say: "What time are you coming home? I'll wait for you to swim with me." I'd walk through the front door and he'd say: "Come on. I've been waiting. Just put everything down and put on your bathing costume. Here it is. You must swim with me."

He made me do things that I wouldn't necessarily have chosen to do, but we had such fun together.

Jamie figured me out very quickly. As soon as he'd learnt to tell the time he'd ask: "Mom, what time are you coming home tonight?" I'd reply: "Seven o'clock." He'd wait for me. He was a real stickler for time. When I walked through the door he'd say: "It is one minute past seven. You're late." I always felt terrible.

As working mothers and career women, we try to do the best in our work life and in our family life, and oftentimes, our children keep us on track. We learn not to make promises that we can't keep. I soon learnt to say: "Okay, tomorrow night, or 'I'll surprise you, I'll come home a little earlier tomorrow night."

Like his dad, Jamie loved animals, especially dogs. We had two German Shepherds and a Jack Russell. I recall looking everywhere for Jamie one day, calling and calling, and getting no response. I eventually found him sitting in the kennel with the three dogs. He smelt very doggy when he emerged from the kennel.

In many ways Jamie was a lot like me. If you gave him a task he'd do it with real passion and focus. It wasn't done until it was done. I recall us laying brick paving in our back yard. The truck deposited a load of bricks in our front garden. Jamie, using his little yellow plastic wheelbarrow, undertook to carry every single brick to the back of the house, one by one.

He'd already moved about fifty bricks and was sweating when I said: "You can stop now. You must take a break." Jamie replied: "No, no, it's not done. I'm busy, I'm working." He had incredible determination, even at such a young age. He was focused on his labours, determined to get things done correctly, to excel.

Jamie loved making a fire. He loved braaiing and he also loved cooking. Whenever his grandfather cooked, you'd find Jamie standing on a chair looking into the pot to see what was going on. And Jamie and I often baked cakes together. Small as he was, he could bake a cake from scratch. It was a case of: "Leave me to do this; just stand there and watch."

He had a flair for cooking. Although you'd never expect this from such a hardy little boy, he won a competition at school for cake decorations. And sushi was his favourite food. The sushi chefs used to come out of the kitchen to look at this young child eating sushi. We always ate it on a Saturday, our special time out together.

Jamie got very excited about things, especially volcanoes. Since Ma Rosy worked for the *Reader's Digest* for many years, we had lots of books with pictures of volcanoes. He'd flick through them almost on a daily basis.

He'd spend months at a time researching volcanoes. He drew pictures of volcanoes and spoke about them like an expert. It was as though there was a scientist sitting inside him ready to emerge with some new theories about volcanoes.

He loved watching the movie, *Volcano*. The movie is about a fault line somewhere in America. Volcanic ash starts to spew out and the lava starts to run onto people. We watched this movie daily for months on end. I must've watched it a hundred times.

There were times when I fell asleep watching the movie, only to be woken by Jamie saying: "We're going to rewind that piece so that we can just see it one more time." I still watch it occasionally because I know how much he loved it.

Jamie struggled with the transition from home to school. We had enrolled him at Woodhill College in Pretoria East, and his grandmother dropped him off in the mornings, but she had to psych him up to get into the car, and psych him up to get out of the car at the other end.

After dropping him off, she had to sit in the car for some time so that he could see the car and her hat. She eventually parked the car and went to the gym up the road. She'd say to him: "You'll see that I'm not in the car. I'm just at the gym up the road and I'll be back."

The problem with school was he was forced to wear shoes and he hated that: he loved being barefoot.

Jamie caught his first fish on 31 December 2002, three days before the accident. We'd visited a trout farm in Paarl, as we were camping at the Berg River. He was very proud of his fish and he wanted me to cook it for him. We took a photograph of Jamie and his fish, and he was wearing the watch we'd given him for Christmas. When we took this photograph, we could never have guessed that we'd use it on the memorial brochure for his funeral, eleven days later.

In 2013 Woodhill College held a memorial service for children in the school who had passed away. The teachers made a beautiful wall of remembrance, with plaques for each of the children. The memorial service was very moving; even more so, since it marked the tenth anniversary of Jamie's passing.

Children bring perspective and new meaning to one's life. There are many life lessons to be learnt through our experience with our child. It was a joy to have him and a devastation to have him pass on.

Kevin and I are so fortunate to have his parents, Ma Jean and Pa Reuben, in our lives. We're deeply indebted to them for all of their love and support over so many years, and especially through the healing period after Jamie's death, when they were grieving the loss of a grandson too.

People often asked me how I managed to live in the same house with my mother-in-law, but all I can say, is that Ma Jean and Pa Reuben are extraordinary people. They were amazing in terms of the help, support, generosity and love they showed Kevin, Jamie and me during this time; and the love and support that they continue to shower upon us. Who else would voluntarily offer to give up their entire social network, leave their family in Cape Town, leave Cape Town itself, which they loved so much, to move with us to Pretoria and help us with Jamie?

The 'in-law' bit is meaningless to me; Ma Jean and Pa Reuben have been, and continue to be like a second set of parents. They stayed with us after Jamie's passing, and only moved back to Cape Town in 2012. We've had so much joy and fun with them. Pa Reuben loves playing dominoes, so he taught Jamie to play, and we used to play dominoes every Sunday night. We cooked together, ate together, and we went away for weekends and holidays together.

Ma Jean and Pa Reuben are very dependable and very caring people. They've played a huge role in terms of what Kevin and I have been able to achieve. They're extraordinary people in their own right. They're generally in good health and are always very optimistic and very curious about what I'm doing, where I'm going, and what is going on in my life. Even today, Ma Jean still looks out for me. She still keeps clippings of articles for me that she thinks I might find interesting, or that I may have missed.

Chapter 11

Healing time

I'd resigned from Reckitt Benckiser to allow myself more time to heal. I'd taken on some small projects, but I still wasn't sure whether I'd ever be able to return to corporate life.

It was during this period that I was approached by a search firm who told me that the Commissioner of South African Revenue Services (SARS), Pravin Gordhan, was looking for a general manager to head up HR. Pravin had already interviewed a number of candidates, but the head-hunter said: "Shirley, just go and see him. Talk to him and decide."

This is exactly what I did. I told Pravin about my personal ordeal over the past few months. I told him I wasn't sure what I was capable of. I'd lost my self-confidence and I was at a low point emotionally. I was brutally honest: I told him I wasn't sure whether I'd be able to drive the major transformation agenda within SARS.

But I realised during our meeting what an amazing leader Pravin Gordhan is. He's passionate about South Africa; he's also passionate about nurturing our fledgling democracy. He has devoted his entire life to making a contribution and building a society based on sound principles and values, and ensuring a better life for all, as enshrined in our Constitution. I was struck by his efficiency and intellectual insights.

Pravin wasn't at all fazed by the challenges that I faced in my personal life, nor by my self-doubt and lack of self-confidence. He asked: "Why don't you think you can do it?"

I replied: "Because I have come through all this."

Pravin responded: "You can do it. When can you start?"

When Pravin offered me the job, it meant so much more to me than merely being employed again. It marked a world of new possibilities and hope after the devastation of losing our only child. My appointment at SARS played a very important role in my recovery. Pravin lifted me up significantly; he built my confidence and he restored my sense of "I can do things."

When I joined SARS, it was at a major turning point in its history. Pravin was implementing massive reforms to bring about a transition from the old regime to a new, high-performing SARS. There were large-scale changes in terms of people, processes and technology. The objective was to ensure that SARS became the efficient and effective tax collection entity that we have today.

As a result of these changes, SARS now combines the functions of the Inland Revenue, and Customs & Excise collections for the Republic of South Africa. Although change is never easy, it was a great honour to be part of these changes.

I truly admire Pravin's leadership ability. He's a passionate, charismatic leader, who played a key role in raising the standards and quality of SARS to a professionally led, citizenry-focused public entity. He had a well-articulated vision and ensured that this translated into the shared experience that we have at SARS today. The vision was to provide an excellent service in a transparent environment, ensuring optimum collection of revenues.

SARS takes its mandate from the Ministry of Finance and this includes the collection and administration of national taxes, duties and levies and protection of the South African economy. It also makes a value-added contribution through its trade facilitation role and administration of partner relationships.

SARS has consistently exceeded its targets and has contributed significantly to the economy, leading to the sustainability of government's fiscal policies, improved cash management, lowering of national budget deficit, and increased investor confidence.

Pravin did this by harnessing all of his people, by putting people first (the *Batho Pele* principle). To convert the motto into reality, SARS launched Siyakha, its own transformation process in February 2000. The organisation's challenge was to monitor the progress of transformation through clearly identified objectives, measures, targets, initiatives and accountabilities.

Pravin's approach was to drive strategic, systematic and intentional change with a view to achieving the strategic goals for a new culture of delivery within SARS. He played a strong communicative role and was highly visible. He was tough and demanded excellence and high performance. He had a solid work ethic and his commitment to change was tangible. He is a true visionary leader.

The organisation's services, business processes and conduct are based on certainty and consistency, equity and fairness, simplicity, integrity and transparency. Pravin always ensured that he was the role model for these values in everything that he did.

In the SARS 2000 annual report Pravin wrote: "The past year has been the most challenging in SARS's history. Not only was a formidable revenue target set, but in February 2000 the Minister of Finance announced the most radical tax policy changes in South Africa's history. At the same time we embarked on an ambitious programme to re-engineer and restructure SARS. I was very privileged to work with the then Minister of Finance, Trevor Manuel, an inspirational leader who has made a huge contribution in the dismantling of apartheid and building our democracy.

"Internally, employees had to adapt to a new grading and remuneration system and a flatter organisational structure, which was a significant departure from the public service legacy – without losing focus on collecting billions of rands and protecting our economy. It has been a tremendous privilege to lead the highly motivated women and men who rose admirably to these challenges and surpassed even their own expectations by year-end."

Not only has Pravin led SARS to stability, he has also led our country to fiscal stability. He went on to become the Minister of Finance and is currently the Minister of Co-operative Governance and Traditional Affairs. He continues to demonstrate great courage, integrity and remains an inspiration to many. It was an honour and a great privilege to work very closely with him. And, committed as I am to social change, transformation and equity, I was very privileged to have played a small role in SARS's transformation.

In the meantime, however, Kevin and I had to deal with the matter of our accident going through the courts. You often hear people saying: "I'll have my day in court." There's a sense that they're expecting some kind of retribution or restitution. At the very least, you want to see that justice has been served.

I'm not a vindictive person, but when something terrible happens, you hope that something positive emerges out of all of the pain, that there's some sense of accountability or responsibility being taken by the perpetrators.

Jamie's case only came to court three years after the accident. As much as we wanted a better understanding of what had happened on that dreadful day, it was extremely painful for Kevin and me, our family and our friends, to have to re-live the horrors of that terrible day through eyewitness accounts and a reconstruction of the accident.

The driver who'd rear-ended our caravan, causing our car and caravan to roll, arrived in court with a battalion of very expensive attorneys. We were given the public prosecutor, who by his own admission had never had to face a case like this before.

Three years after the accident documents had to emerge and eyewitnesses had to be found. This process is flawed, and reasons for such delays are never given. Hearing a trial based on the recollections of eyewitnesses so long after the event reduces the likelihood of a fair trial, especially if the defendant can afford a very good legal team.

The driver of the vehicle was only twenty-one at the time of the accident. I said to him: "If it really was an accident then please just say so and we can all just get on with our lives. I don't harbour any ill towards you." He was acquitted because of a lack of sufficient evidence. I don't know whether he ever gives the accident any thought, or whether the accident has changed his life in any way. I've never seen or heard from him since.

But Kevin and I were determined to move forward with our lives. This wasn't necessarily closure, but it was a clear decision that this was the end of that chapter. We were going to find a way to move on in a constructive manner. Although it will always be with us, we weren't going to carry around the bitterness and the pain and those bad memories of what happened on that dreadful day.

When we think of Jamie we don't think of the accident. We think about a lovely little boy who had lots of energy. He bought a lot of fun and joy into our lives. This is what we think about, not the sadness of having lost him and that he's not here to live his full life.

Jamie taught us some key lessons. I've learnt that children are really gifts. We can't demarcate hours of the day and say: "This makes me a good mother or a good parent." You have to be good all of the time, whether you're at work, or whether you're at home, whether you're a 24/7 mother or whether you work outside the home from nine to five. We have to be good in terms of when we're with them. We have to ensure that we give them the quality time, the attention, the love, the security, the care, the joy of life that they need. We must ensure that we are able to provide all of these things, all of the time.

I don't believe in the notion that I'm a working mother and I need to balance my life by spending two hours here and three hours there. I believe in living a meaningful life and making sure that we're being the very best we can be on all fronts. This is a tough ask in a fast-paced world, where everyone has to be in high performance mode all the time.

Mothers, you don't have to feel guilty when you quietly crawl out of the office at five o'clock to pick up your child or participate in an extramural activity. We lay this guilt on ourselves because society has designed all sorts of frameworks within which we're supposed to live our lives that often don't make sense.

We put ourselves under so much undue pressure when we could just be great parents and great mothers in our own right without feeling that someone is watching the clock all the time. I'm very privileged to have had seven years with such an outstanding little human being. I think my life would've been far less aspirational and inspirational if I didn't have the benefit of having this child.

People often ask: "Did you ever think of having another child?" It took Kevin and me a long time to work through what had happened to us. You can never replace a child. I sometimes think that perhaps I should've worked harder at having more children when I was able to do so.

After Jamie's death I went for a few sessions of in-vitro fertilisation. I had two miscarriages: I lost one baby in the first miscarriage and twins in the second – that was the end of trying to have children biologically. We thought about adoption, but decided to move on.

It's hard to imagine that if things had worked out the way we'd have liked, I'd be the mother of four children. But I've laid this to rest. Had Jamie survived the accident, he might have had some severe challenges, so I've often chosen to support children with disabilities.

I'm the chairman of the Starfish Foundation, which channels funding to orphaned and vulnerable children. We make sure that these children get an education, health services and the protection they deserve.

I've been able to be a mother in a different way. It's not coincidental that the work that I've been privileged to do for many years as an educator and as an HR director in large organisations has enabled me to help many thousands of people. I've been able to help them create better lives, create joy in their lives and helped them thrive even in difficult circumstances.

Sometimes, just in telling our story, in talking about our loss, we see people realising our common humanity. We often forget about this when we talk about diversity issues and different struggles around race or gender, or any other differences people may have.

We're all just human beings, trying to come to terms with the human condition. Once you've stripped yourself of titles and status and rank, we're all just navigating a journey on this planet as best we possibly can. We all have our setbacks, challenges, victories and celebrations. We need to find ways to derive happiness and joy in a way that makes sense in terms of our own definition of what happiness and joy really is all about.

Having Jamie in our lives taught us the sheer joy of living life to the hilt, living every day not as if it's your last day, but living every day just because it's a gift that we get to open our eyes every day and think about the possibilities and opportunities that life is going to bring our way.

So, despite all of the sadness and all of the loss, I remain very optimistic. I remain very excited about the difference I can make in the lives of the people around me. This gives me meaning and purpose every day.

CHAPTER 12

BACK INTO CORPORATE LIFE

In December 2003, Tom Boardman was appointed CEO of Nedbank and in 2005 he approached me to join his team as the head of HR.

Although this was a very exciting opportunity, it was also very daunting. Nedbank was facing some very challenging times: headline earnings were down ninety-eight percent and return on equity was only 0.4%. Market capitalisation was the lowest of the 'big four' – South Africa's four biggest banks. Old Mutual had to recapitalise the bank so it injected R2-billion in primary capital and raised an additional R5.2-billion through a rights issue.

Market sentiment was very negative, staff morale was low, the organisational culture was dysfunctional, there was no clearly articulated vision and strategy, and confidence levels among the senior leadership at Nedbank were very low.

Tom had the mammoth task of delivering on a financial turnaround at a time when the media were having a field day. During the first discussion I had with Tom, he said something deeply profound that persuaded me to seriously consider the opportunity he had put before me. He said that he would not be able to do the financial turnaround without the people. I was blown over by this as I have heard many CEOs paying lip service to the idea that their people are the greatest asset in the business. Tom really meant it.

Tom's vision for the bank was: "To become Southern Africa's most highly rated and respected bank ... by our staff, clients, shareholders, regulators and communities." His philosophy was straight out of *Alice in Wonderland*, courtesy of the Cheshire Cat: "If you don't know where you are going then any road will take you there."

We all knew it was an enormous challenge. At the time Nedbank employed twenty-seven thousand people – very concerned people who were anxious about the envisaged changes. Staff morale was low; belief in the new leadership was yet to be established.

But Tom is a great leader. He understood the importance of leaders taking their people along with them as they worked towards the same goal and vision. He also understood that a financial turnaround would not be possible without boosting staff morale, and aligning their vision and values with those of management.

Working at Nedbank brought me an enormous sense of fulfilment at a professional level. We achieved the financial turnaround in 2008, successfully managed by Tom, who was values-led and vision driven. He understood that people are the key to business success. He's a transformational leader who won the respect of his staff, clients, and community. He had a way of taking people along with him, and he also had a strong, collaborative spirit.

Tom believed in courageous conversations: conversations that tackle the difficult aspects of corporate life. But the problem with courageous conversations is that some things make people very vulnerable. You're forced to drop your guard and reveal who you really are.

We were able to do this very successfully at Nedbank. This is why the bank was able to move through that three-year financial turnaround in the way that it did. People really started to connect with others in ways in they'd never been able to previously.

You can have an academic relationship with someone; you can also have a professional relationship. However, if we're trying to be a team, I need to know who I'm working with. I need to know what makes you tick, what you think, and why you behave as you do. I also need to know what I should or shouldn't do if I want to get things done. We need to have more of these conversations, but very few people are prepared to have them.

The Nedbank culture required us, as the leadership, to share a lot of ourselves. Not many organisations do this. Colleagues provided feedback through three hundred and sixty degree reviews. While these reviews revealed our gaps, they also helped us build on our strengths and improve in areas where we weren't great.

One of the important lessons that I've learnt is that it's quite okay to have strengths and weaknesses – or areas for development as they are often euphemistically labelled. You cannot be good at everything and shouldn't beat yourself up if you're not good at something. I've learnt to play to my strengths. I've also learnt to accept feedback.

Tom once commented: "Shirley, you need to learn to say 'no' more often. The only reason that I'm telling you this is that I'm a lot like you in this respect." Here was a CEO, who was also my boss, giving me this feedback in front of my colleagues. I had to agree with Tom's assessment and take this on board, and look to my colleagues to help me in this regard. I am still working on this.

There are things that you know you do well. There are also things that need to be handed over to someone else to do, and this shouldn't be seen as failure. There are no super-people around, there are only people who do things well, and who keep trying to do things better. Tom believed feedback was about continuous learning. He believed learning is never wasted: at some stage in your life it will be useful.

Tom had held significant roles in his career, and he shared some of the lessons he'd learned with us, his leadership team. He was very aware of the importance of organisational culture and its impact on business success. He also displayed strong people-orientation. He showed tenacity, resilience and focus through challenging times.

We spoke about 'liberating the soul of the organisation' and that 'organisations don't change, people do'. Both ideas come from the work of Richard Barrett, and they helped to get people re-engaged and passionate about the organisation.

But Tom had to retire from Nedbank in 2009 and as the Head of HR for Nedbank at the time I had to help find a successor. This was critical as the bank's sustainability hinged on appointing the right person. Mike Brown was appointed as CEO of Nedbank in 2009. He'd been the CFO of the bank up to that point and I believe that Mike was the very best successor to Tom.

I was so busy at Nedbank, that the thought of going to work for a competitor bank never crossed my mind. The inconceivable happened: in 2010 Standard Bank approached me to become head of HR in South Africa, and deputy global head of HR for the group. Elizabeth Warren and Sim Tshabalala were very persuasive.

This was a compelling proposition. I was aware that if I wanted to progress in my career, I would have to take on a global role. Standard Bank offered me the opportunity to work in a global bank, based in Johannesburg. Kevin and I had many conversations about whether I should do this, given that I was very happy at Nedbank and loved working there, but after much soul-searching and weighing up the odds of working a global environment without leaving the country, I decided to move across to Standard Bank.

I started at Standard Bank on 4 October 2010. Days before I joined the bank, the Standard Bank board had already taken a decision to retrench two thousand employees. I knew nothing about this decision before I joined, and it's the hardest thing I've ever faced in my career. There is a huge difference between the paper exercise and the reality of terminating people's employment contracts, knowing that their future financial security is uncertain.

Coming from the Cape Flats, where life is a struggle, I was very aware of the impact that retrenchment can have on families. I knew that people can lose their homes, their cars, families often split up, and couples get divorced because of financial difficulties. I also knew that retrenchment could impact very negatively on an individual's sense of self-worth and self-esteem.

I spent many a sleepless night because of the wide-scale retrenchments that I had to implement with my team. I love working in HR, because I love developing people. I don't like losing staff or asking them to leave, especially when performance is not the issue. Often these are 'business decisions', and have to be implemented because areas of the business have changed operationally. They are difficult to implement nonetheless.

Leadership can be a very lonely place at the best of times; it is even lonelier when you have to do something that might have been done differently. I made my feelings known to the board, but unfortunately they'd made up their minds, and there was no scope for me to explore alternative options.

Many of my friends saw the toll that this was taking on me personally. "You don't have to do this," they said to me. "You don't want that job." I never believed anything like this could happen to me. By telling my story, I hope I'll be able to help others through complex situations such as this.

It takes people a long time to overcome the devastation of having to leave a company when it's not their choice to do so. It's also very difficult for those who stay behind, to retain their focus and overcome the emotional setback of losing colleagues they worked with for so many years. These processes have to be thoughtfully and carefully implemented.

I've learnt that when dealing with people, dignity and humility are of paramount importance. And once the retrenchment process had been completed, I had to focus on rebuilding certainty and hope in those who continued without their retrenched colleagues.

The long hours, the difficult conversations, the emotions of the people, the documentation and the reporting on progress were intense and demanding. Christmas 2010 came and went as we tried to move this very difficult process to conclusion.

My time with family and friends was very limited, and I was constantly preoccupied with he challenges at work. By the time 2012 came, time was ticking towards the tenth anniversary of Jamie's passing.

This made me think even harder about the meaning of life. It took its toll on me, and led me to deeply reflect on choices I would need to make very soon thereafter. The question of how we might motivate and inspire the remaining staff was huge. We also needed to improve engagement and productivity that naturally takes a dive during processes like this. Most of my time for the next twelve months was spent on creating further efficiencies and effectiveness, and supporting the re-architecturing of the bank.

Kevin was also concerned about my health and well-being through this challenging time and supported the view that I needed a break from corporate life, or some sort of sabbatical. It was not easy to have these conversations about leaving the bank with my colleagues. I was quite emotional about leaving and taking a break from corporate life, a life I had become accustomed to and understood so well, especially when I wasn't too sure about what might come next.

But when the time was right, I was ready to move on to the next challenge, which included spending more quality time with loved ones, catching up on things deferred and postponed, and, most of all, reinventing myself. I decided to leave the bank in September 2012 and revive my own small business, combining all the wisdom of decades of study and work experience. We also decided to move back to Cape Town to be closer to family, especially our ageing parents.

Reviving Shirley Zinn Consulting has been the most revitalising experience. Amazingly, it was Kevin's idea back in 2003 for me to register my own company. For a decade he tried to coax me into starting my own consulting company; he had more faith in me than I had in myself. He always spoke confidently about how I would not just succeed but soar.

Shirley Zinn Consulting was not the lesser option; it's about a new, exciting chapter in my life, where I do things on my terms, where I strike the balance that works for me at this stage in my life, and where I'm able to explore new and exciting opportunities that could emerge.

I really enjoyed the complexity of Standard Bank. I was both impressed and somewhat daunted by the bank's global reach into thirty-three countries. And I was also excited by its proclaimed strategic intention to grow its footprint into Africa, where it had already established its presence in seventeen countries. I enjoyed the intellectual stretch and the many challenges that came my way. The joy of working in HR is really about seeing people grow and thrive in their lives, including their careers.

The last few decades have been intense and varied. I've grown and I've learnt a great deal. I share some of the most important lessons that I've learnt in the chapters that follow.

The interesting thing about life is that every complexity that confronts us is a building block for a new opportunity. We need to learn to relish those moments when we find ourselves swimming upstream. It's during times like these that we learn and grow the most. Without being stretched to our limits, how can we possibly know what we are capable of?

Because if my life has demonstrated anything, it's that you don't have to remain trapped in the circumstances of your birth. You have to determine your future. That's the message I have for young people like me who are growing up in places where poverty is rife and opportunities are few.

There are many places that you can go to for help. There are many counselling services and community NGOs – use them! Use all of the help that is available to you. Never be too proud to ask for help. There are times when you'll need to put your pride in your pocket, and the fact that I've been able to uplift myself from the circumstances I was born into, is living evidence that it can be done.

Chapter 13

What it takes

There are a lot of misconceptions out there about what it takes to be a successful businesswoman, but I know from personal experience that it's possible to conquer the boardroom in stilettos. It's possible to crack that glass ceiling: set your sights high and aim for that apex. I refused to allow myself to be defined by the concept of a glass ceiling.

I've never assumed a particular persona, been something I'm not, said anything I don't believe in, or said something I haven't thought through properly. I've always been respectful of the views of others and I've never emulated male behaviour to get a few steps ahead. I have worked with men who believed in gender equity and that we need to build a society based on principles of equity and fairness together as men and women.

I love being a woman, and I celebrate my femininity in ways that work for me: I take great care with my make-up, I dress for the occasion, I try to make an impression when I walk in that I'm 'all woman'. I see my femininity as a key strength, and I can only seek to be the best version of myself.

Women need to be allowed to be women; they need to be respected for who they are. We need to create a better South Africa – a better world – for all and we need to ensure that all are included: black, white, male and female. All of us must benefit from the democracy that we're trying to build where men and women can flourish in an inclusive, fair and just society.

The spirit of our Constitution, of unity in diversity, isn't about displacing any group of people. Neither is the spirit of *ubuntu*, and it certainly wasn't Madiba's vision that we do so. For me the philosophy around gender and equality is about creating inclusivity and an integrated society premised on the principles of democracy and a better life for all.

In my HR role, I realised that hiring diverse talent is one of the biggest challenges that leaders face today, given the global war for talent. The best mix and diversity of talent translates into diversity of thinking, optimal performance and provides organisations with a real, tangible, measurable competitive edge. Many organisations, however, simply don't get the mix and diversity of talent right, but are happy to tick the boxes for the sake of compliance.

They also fail to harness and unleash the potential in their people by pigeonholing and boxing people in, or labelling them and telling them there are certain things they can and can't do.

Individuals are also guilty of this by placing huge limitations on themselves, when they think they can only do so much. We sometimes think we need to be an Einstein to add value, but this really isn't the case. Often, the little incremental things we do have a huge impact and there are many things that we have to do for the first time.

South Africa is desperately trying to grow its economy, and we need to harness the talent of every single person, male, female, white or black, to ensure that we're effectively growing this country to compete in the global environment, in line with our national vision as expressed in the National Development Plan. Women constitute fifty-two percent of the population, and we simply cannot be dismissive of fifty-two percent of the talent in this country.

We need male and female leaders who can achieve this in both the public and private spheres. The more we can get the best and the brightest people into our organisations – irrespective of race and gender – the better.

Having said this, we still need to correct the past. We need to find a way to unlock economic liberation for people and find ways to harness the collective intellect of all people in this country. We must put them into positions of leadership and give them opportunities that they might never have had.

If we're able to do this, South Africa will be a much better place, much sooner than if we spin our wheels and have endless debates that don't go anywhere. Many of our debates about transformation are about compliance, tick boxes and numbers. We have lost the spirit of what we are really trying to achieve through economic empowerment.

As women, we also need to recognise the men who've made a difference in our lives. I've been fortunate to have had friends, colleagues, a husband and a father, including leaders like Tom Boardman and Pravin Gordhan, who've all displayed enormous generosity of spirit in allowing and enabling me to do the things that I've done. They've all supported me in a very real way.

I've always had great men around me. I intentionally surrounded myself all my life around good men. I subscribe fully to UNICEF's definition of gender equality: "Gender equality means that women and men, boys and girls enjoy the same rights, resources, opportunities and protections ... it does not require that they be treated exactly alike."[2]

I also subscribe to Wendy Harcourt's views, expressed in the Report on World Commission on Culture and Development 1995: "The time is past when a women's movement had to exclude men in the fight against patriarchy. The time has come rather for women's vision to restructure and redefine work in order to fashion a new society for women and men based on women's experience and skills as care-givers and reproducers."

---

2   http://www.unicef.org/mdg/files/Overarching_2Pager_Web.pdf (accessed 28 July 2015)

Some women actively seek out like-minded women: I've never done so. I draw on the strengths of everyone around me for moving the organisation forward and I try to take people along with me, even if we differ on some points.

Besides ticking the boxes from a legal and compliance point of view, research shows that where women are on boards and in senior executive positions, organisations have a better triple bottom line. I've always wanted my brain-power to work for me.

But while I believe that women play a huge role in board and senior management positions, I'm always very careful not to state emphatically what qualities women bring to the boardroom or to senior management. This can lead to stereotyping. You don't want to see women defined by a cadre of leadership that does the soft stuff. You want to see women, together with men, being able to build a great organisation that is successful.

Women make a huge difference when they're empowered to do what they need to do within the organisation. Smart organisations have worked this out. When you interpret this in a systematic and thoughtful way, you can realise results you never imagined possible.

It's not always perfect, but as a general principle, in a world where talent is in such short supply at decision-making levels, you cannot possibly exclude half of your candidates. Women such as Oprah Winfrey, Gloria Serobe, Maria Ramos, and Graça Machel have stepped up even when they've had to stand alone. There are women on our own continent who've played a great role and have made a huge difference, not just to organisations, but to society. These women have to be celebrated.

It's important to acknowledge that while we need to create gender equity in the workplace and in society as a whole, we still face many challenges and deep-seated prejudices. Women have been socialised to be subservient, so when women step up and want to have their voices heard they're often seen to be too aggressive, too outspoken, and too pushy. Paternalistic behaviour is still very much alive and well.

We live our lives within a broader environment, within a society that has decided to structure and frame itself based on things that are acceptable, and things that aren't. We have all kinds of unwritten rules and intangibles that sometimes play themselves out in the most horrific way in boardrooms and engagements in the workplace.

It's also important to acknowledge that women are socialised as little girls to be polite, nice, subservient, co-operative and accommodating, so we sometimes struggle with the notion of being feminine and being ambitious at the same time. The challenge is that we have to compete in the world as it's currently set up. We have to come to terms with personal ambition and not be defensive or apologetic about our aspirations.

I'm currently coaching a woman whose boss has told her that when she speaks out she's too "aggressive". He actually used that word in his brief to me. If it were a man speaking like this, it would be acceptable. When women do the same thing, however, they try to silence you or take you out, which is what they tried to do in this case.

Women often find themselves in this position because someone, perhaps even their boss, thinks they're a little too confident. The confidence is identified as being ambition. It's never a case of 'she's done her homework', 'she knows what she's doing', or 'she has a point' and she is a valued member of the team.

Many women suffer emotional abuse at work and at home, the fall-out being depression, anxiety and decreased morale. You can't always choose your boss, but you don't have to take abuse. You have the right to respectfully and professionally disagree, and to reserve your rights if need be.

There are, however, many men who've understood this and who accept that equity is required. We need to recognise our common humanity as men and women, and that we need to co-exist and build a meaningful future together.

We need to engage men and women in the equality and mainstreaming dialogue; we also need to make men accountable for gender equity. This isn't a women-only issue, but a societal and economic issue to make everyone financially sustainable and contribute to overall economic growth and prosperity.

South Africa is still without adequate representation of women in JSE-listed corporations, reports the Businesswomen's Association of South Africa (BWASA) in the 2015 South African Women in Leadership Census. It is very concerning that only 8.79% of JSE-listed companies have twenty-five percent or more women directors (BWASA 2015). The research conducted also draws on international benchmarks and cites South Africa as a top performer amongst BRICS countries, with almost double the percentage of women directors, compared to its nearest competitor, China (at 11.1%).

There is a concern that although there are more women than men now graduating with degrees, women are still pursuing degrees in non-critical disciplines as per the country's skills requirements. We are beneficiaries and guardians of our Bill of Rights and have a collective responsibility to ensure that all women benefit from this. We, both men and women in this country, have to continue to be activists for change and equality. The job is never really done, and we could regress if we take our eye off the ball.

We especially need to pay attention to rural development, as women in these environments have endured even further marginalisation economically and socially. Our big enemy is our history of gender inequality and social engineering. We are not confronting this sufficiently, and superficial, peripheral efforts will not be sustainable. We need to collectively drive systemic solutions that will permeate public policy, organisational practices and social responsibility to ensure that justice prevails.

We require a convergence of both public sector, private sector and civil society to focus on what will make South Africa great. We need to unify our nation around a single vision, and embrace the notion that social stability and national cohesion precede economic growth.

Our personal contributions to equality should not be underestimated. We are called upon in the South African National Development Plan to be "active citizens" and to make the changes in society that are enshrined in our Constitution. We need to shape the values and behaviours in our families, communities and society through dialogue, debate, education and personal accountability for change.

The fact is that life is harder for women than men all over the world. Society, in general, still engages in economic, social and political discrimination and inequities continue to pervade our life experiences. The lists of challenges and atrocities that women face as a result, are endless. Many of these have been documented, but for most women, their stories remain locked in the silence of prejudice and pain.

Even after twenty years of democracy in South Africa, the struggle for gender inequality continues. We need systemic solutions; we cannot simply leave it up to women to fix the societal ills of discrimination against women.

As I write this book, we are celebrating Women's Month in South Africa. On 9 August 2015 we marked twenty years since our country began celebrating National Women's Day. On 9 August 1956, the non-racial Federation of South African Women (FEDSAW) organised twenty thousand women, who marched to the Union Buildings in Pretoria to present a petition against the carrying of passes by women to the then Prime Minister, JG Strijdom. The courage of these women to rise up against apartheid rule is key to our struggle for democracy.

In South Africa, we have the double-header of gender and race discrimination. There might even be a triple-header if we include poverty and marginalisation of women to the periphery of the economy. Sexism is a reality in our society as well as business.

We have so many laws in South Africa promoting gender equity, especially at the higher levels of organisations. We know, however, that laws are only one enabling element; it's not necessarily only about the law but about behaviour. It is going to take a long time to achieve parity.

A lot of work has been done indicating that where women are on boards there is a huge increase in the bottom line. The research institute of Swiss banking group Credit Suisse surveyed the share price and overall performance of more than two thousand four hundred companies from

2005 over a six-year period. Companies with at least some female board representation outperformed those that didn't have any women on the board. Large cap stocks performed more than twenty-six percent better (*Daily Maverick*, February 2013).

Having women in leadership roles isn't just in the company's best interest from a bottom line perspective – it also makes a broader societal difference. Talent is a major consideration: the biggest conundrum for leaders today is the hiring of top talent and they cannot afford to ignore women.

But while the glass ceiling has some cracks in it, there still aren't enough women at the top. Furthermore, the wage and welfare gaps remain for the majority of women, and even though women are getting into the C-suite, there is sometimes an indifference to them, an inability to meaningfully include them, and a tokenistic attitude towards them.

Women who want to make it to the top of the corporate ladder, you need to know that you will need a great deal of tenacity; you will also be required to swim upstream. You need to have self-confidence and self-belief to succeed, Build your personal brand – plan, focus and make it happen, avoiding analysis paralysis and being overly self-critical. It is important that you surround yourself with inspirational people.

There is a choice that women make about whether they're willing to continue up into the C-suite or whether they actually want to step down and do something completely different before they reach retirement age.

Women often consciously 'off-ramp'[3] in their careers, because they reach a point where they say, "No more of this corporate life." Many of them take the time out to give birth and raise their children, and many of them don't go back to corporates, but do very well as entrepreneurs.

We don't always know about them, because their success stories are seldom published. Some do return to corporate life and are initially challenged by the re-integration, as this is not always a well-entrenched practice within corporates. Many progress well and go on to achieve great things in their careers and more broadly, in their lives.

---

3   *Off-Ramps and On-Ramps: Keeping Talented Women on the Road to Success* by Sylvia Ann Hewlett and Carolyn Buck Luce in the Harvard Business Review, March 2005.

But having said all of this, there are great stories of women who have succeeded, of companies who have excelled at gender mainstreaming. We need to celebrate these women and hear their stories so that we might be inspired and learn from them.

When I reflect on the most recent part of my journey, I know that I was daunted about what lay ahead when I left Standard Bank. However, I knew that I needed to take the time out after about thirty years of very hard work. And I also knew that it wasn't going to be easy to break into a market that I'm not familiar with. But I knew that I had a bundle of strengths and experiences that I could re-package and present into the market when I was ready.

I've been blown away by the responses that I've had so far. I've had multiple clients and a variety of different projects. These are all about shifting hearts and minds in their organisations – change management, transformation and inclusion, and leadership development. I love the work I do. It gives me an enormous sense of personal fulfilment to know that I am making a difference.

I've had the opportunity to work very closely with CEOs, MDs and some HR directors on various complex projects. I have done a bit of advisory work, and hopefully it is high impact: as high impact as it might have been if I was the HR director or chief HR officer in any other organisation.

But transitions are not easy and there are clear risks involved. You have to be mindful of this. The point is that it is possible to repackage yourself: there are things that you can do differently. Some of us just stay in the same space because we just are so daunted by what other people think we can and can't do. We become a recluse stuck in an unfulfilling place as opposed to liberating ourselves to do more meaningful and greater things.

If I ever went back into corporate life, an option I have not yet entirely ruled out, I know with absolute certainty that I would be able to add so much more value because of what I've been through as an entrepreneur. I have learnt that ordinary people can do extraordinary things.

Chapter 14

THE BOARDROOM – WHERE GOOD GOVERNANCE SHOULD PREVAIL

The boardroom is the place where good governance should prevail, but it is often a battle ground where different ideas, ideologies, agendas, often dysfunctional relationships, personalities, and alliances come into play as decisions are made. Conflict levels can be very high and you can find yourself having to deal with some very unpleasant and uncomfortable situations. There's also a lot of bullying, and men and women are equally guilty of this.

It's not in your best interest to bang your fist on the table to be heard in the boardroom. Do your homework and think very carefully about what you say, when to say it and how to best say it. Put on the table what is always backed by research, preparation and experience.

I allow people to bounce around what I've said, agree or disagree with parts, and I've always been very professional in my approach. And even during the most trying times, I've always retained my composure.

But a lot of it is just bravado and heroics, the drama of the board and the dynamics of "What's in it for me? How persuasive can I be in this scenario? Am I in a position to influence the debate and add value in this scenario?" Sometimes people lose why they're there. They forget that their commitment is oversight of the business, and making sure that it is successful. Instead they get involved in issues with individuals around the table that are counterproductive to the business.

Board members often lack the emotional maturity to be able to broach difficult subjects, to facilitate the movement of complex negotiation, or the ability to spot a storm brewing and trying to intervene in time. Unfortunately, board training only includes the technicalities of how boards work, the legalities and the fiduciary duties; there's a dire need to include the behavioural and attitudinal requirements.

It's inevitable that people will differ with you on certain issues, but this shouldn't be seen as something negative, nor should it be taken personally. Rather, it's an opportunity for robust debate and to persuade others in a compelling way, or to listen carefully and give up on your viewpoint as there are better views on the table.

I often come across as quiet and concerned about the soft issues of leading people and some might think it would be easy to sway me. But I'm willing to step in and step up boldly when it is necessary. I always ensure that my opinion is heard. I'm not aggressive or loud, but if I differ or disagree with you, I will make my point as best I can or accept alternative thoughts that might be better than mine if I am persuaded.

You really don't have to be a bull in a china shop to get your point across. You can do things with conviction, in a compelling way, in a way that is sufficiently descriptive to take people on a different thought trajectory.

But you also need to be tactful, because people don't always see where you're going. We sometimes lose tact in the rough and tumble, especially when we respond emotionally.

I try to use tact to redirect people to the general purpose, to get there with minimal disruptions. There are times, however, when disruption is necessary. If things aren't going to work, you need to say: "Let's do something else."

A lot of conflict could be resolved if people just listened, observed and noticed how people are feeling about what's going on. Listening is such an important leadership capability. We could get to a point where we could meaningfully resolve issues if more people realised that board fall-outs are often the result of people not listening to one another.

Whenever people disagree with me I always listen very intently to what they're saying. The ability to listen and actually hear where others are coming from, in other words, to put myself in their shoes, especially if we disagree on an issue, has stood me in good stead.

If I'm wrong I'm also prepared to step back, concede and apologise. There is give and take in all things. This is something that people sometimes forget. We can be very ambitious about our own agenda, but we need to listen and give credit where it is due.

I've also learnt that people often try to provoke you – we all have emotional triggers. I'm no Miss Goody Two Shoes, who never does anything wrong and never goes off the rails. Self-awareness is another important leadership capability as it really defines who you are, how you respond to people and understand your impact on others.

Values are very important to me: integrity, respect, honesty, and openness have always been hallmarks of how I've wanted to build my life. I've always wanted to live an ethical life, so I have difficulties when people say one thing and do another, or when they fail to apologise when they're out of line, or they undermine my values. I'm very aware of the fact that these are emotional triggers for me.

But you need to guard against being provoked and losing your temper. There are times when I get angry, but I always try to step back, take stock and understand. There are times when I've said: "I cannot respond to that right now. I want to mull over things, but I hear what you're saying."

Acknowledge that some people cannot reconcile with certain types of people. You're bound to have a conflict and it's how you are going to engage with the matter and resolve it that's important. In life there are many people that we don't like, and most times we don't even know why.

The question is, do we want to be liked or respected?

Some people are deeply operational and they're very passionate about what they do. Tell them to cut costs and they'll spend their time doing just that. Then you have people who are strategic. They're thinking five years ahead. They understand that they must cut costs, but they're also thinking way ahead of the game about how to grow and build the business. If you put two people like this in a room, they might go past one another until they realise that they are both acting in the best interest of the business.

As leaders, it's important to notice what's happening in the room, including the board room. It's important to help people to understand what's happening so that we can all move along. We need more courageous leadership, leaders who are able to speak out and facilitate processes. We need leaders who are able to nip conflict in the bud and move people back to productive engagement. We need leaders who can resolve problems before they become a crisis.

I always try to take the emotion out of things, and try to listen so that I might respond effectively, and rationally, rather than impulsively. When the going gets tough I'm guided by Martin Luther King's words: "The ultimate measure of a man is not when he stands in moments of comfort and convenience, but when he stands at times of challenge and controversy."

While I was at Harvard I spent time with Paulo Freire, the influential Brazilian educator, philosopher, advocate of critical pedagogy and author of *Pedagogy of the Oppressed*. One of the things I learnt from him is that reflection is very important before action, and that you need to review your actions, before stepping up into the next action if you are to learn and continuously improve what you do.

Today, in the world of business, we don't always have the time to think and to think deeply. Deep thinking should inform whether you step into something or whether you step away from something. You can't step up every time; stepping in has its own risks and dangers. Sometimes you have to step away in order to move forward.

So I always encourage people to think before they leap. Everything, especially in business, is moving at a fast pace. Senior executives often say, as they rush from pillar to post, that there isn't time to think. They rush through meetings, they don't always do their homework, and they don't always prepare their minds properly. There is insufficient readiness; they haven't tilled the ground sufficiently and don't know what territory they're entering into. The danger is that one can be busy without being productive.

This doesn't mean you must hesitate every time. It's not about hesitation, and it's not about always imagining the risk to be so high that you're paralysed by the thought of being decisive. It's really just taking the time out to ask: "Is this the right direction and I am doing the right thing?"

It's about checking it out, making sure your diagnostics are right, making sure your dashboard is showing the right signs. It's about making sure you're seeing the opportunity that no-one else has seen, and stepping into it on time.

Volumes have been written about what it takes to be a great leader. While the theory is all very well, the acid test for leadership lies in the actual doing. It's about leaders being able to take their people along with them.

I've been very privileged to work very closely with three great business leaders: Aletha Ling, Pravin Gordhan and Tom Boardman. Aletha, Pravin and Tom taught me that vision, values, attitude and behaviour are critical for effective leadership. They also taught me that effective leadership is about having the ability to inspire hope and to take people along with you. A good balance of empathy and compassion, and the ability to have the tough conversations, are important leadership attributes.

It's about understanding your impact on others, caring, nurturing stewardship, being confident without losing humility, succeeding despite the setbacks and the odds, continuous learning, making a stand for what you believe in (even if you stand alone), simplifying and adaptability, relationships with people (staff, clients, community), service to people, and viewing obstacles as opportunities waiting to be unleashed.

Leadership is also about ethics and having a moral compass, about empowerment rather than control and command and instilling fear and anxiety, being aware of your impact on others, emotional intelligence, and the ability to unify organisations and create convergence of thought toward a common goal.

A well-rounded leader is able to influence and able to persuade, she's also able to 'walk the talk'. A well-rounded leader has a social conscience. A well-rounded leader continually thinks about how she is able to make a difference in the world and run a successful business.

Being a good leader is about being connected to the pulse of your organisation and what is going on with your people. It's about being able to shift whatever is happening within the organisation into a better, more meaningful space. Pravin and Tom's work in transforming SARS and Nedbank respectively, are very good examples of this.

Leadership is also about being selfless. It's about being of service, not just to your organisation in a selfish way, but in the spirit of the triple bottom line – people, planet and profit – and thinking about how you can sustain your staff and the communities in which you do business.

Well-rounded leaders take care of themselves. They stay healthy, they stay fit, they eat well. Ever now and then my husband reminds me to take some personal time out: time to take care of myself by going to sleep earlier and enjoying a longer sleep-in because it's the weekend, to go to gym to re-energise my mind and body, to enjoy a slow sunset walk with him without talking any shop at all, or laugh out aloud at a ridiculous movie on TV. He continues to remind me nearly daily that without good health you have nothing.

Great leaders are also family and community people. They have good emotional intelligence (EQ) – undoubtedly one of the most powerful weapons in the suite of leadership capital, yet probably the least understood.

Emotional intelligence stems from one's vision and values, and it's about the ability to assess what is actually happening, what the dynamics are, who is saying what to whom. It's also about asking yourself what response you will get if you say what you want to say five minutes later rather than responding immediately without thinking it through in a mindful way. Good EQ is about saying: "If I'm listening to you, connecting with you, we might be able to get to a better place."

EQ has played a very important role in my own success. It has enabled me to understand people, build meaningful relationships, connect with people, get people to effectively change behaviours, to do things that they might not have done otherwise, and to think things they might not have thought otherwise.

Much of my personal success emanates from my ability to figure out what's really going on: to be discerning, to understand the underlying dynamics and to work out what to say, when to say it, how to say it, and whether or not to say it.

The ability to build connectivity, to influence and shape the dialogue, and to leave a mark, is premised on EQ. I've always been well endowed with the ability to connect with people, to help uncover the nugget that nobody else was able to find, to give hope and to inspire. I'd like to stress, however, that when building networks one should always seek to build meaningful relationships with people. Networks should never be abused for personal gain.

One of the issues we don't talk about enough is the fact that there's a time when it's good for a leader to leave. When Tom Boardman's succession plan was completed and he had to leave, at his final speech he said that it is as important to leave as well and as elegantly as you arrived.

Sometimes in the leaving, you leave in a way that gets people to ask all the wrong questions. For me the art of quitting is very important. Many leaders don't know when to do this. We've seen examples of this worldwide, including on our own continent. Leaders sometimes hold onto power and onto pieces of a dream. This can be detrimental for the country or for the organisation.

By remaining in a position for too long, leaders become counter-productive, static and they often operate on cruise control. They lose their ability to innovate and give direction. They may even cut off opportunities for others in their quest to hold onto a position, or hold onto power.

Knowing when to quit and knowing how to quit is critical. We've seen examples of leaders who have worked their way up into amazing careers. Our former and beloved president, Nelson Mandela, is a good example of a leader who knew when it was time to leave. He refused to stand for another term of office, as he recognised that it was important to hand over the baton to new leadership.

When you get to a point where you need to make a decision, all the signs will be there. You need to be in tune with what is going on in the environment. You need to listen to what employees are saying, to what your client is saying, and to what the market is saying. You need to take this into account and do the honourable thing at the right time.

Chapter 15

Being innovative

Innovation is widely acknowledged as a differentiator and a critical success factor in business today. Being innovative means surrounding yourself with a diverse array of people, who think differently about the world. By listening to, and harvesting the different voices within the organisation, one is able to pull together the gems and ask: "What is the best and most interesting way forward?"

Smart organisations know that the intellectual capacity of their people to come up with new and innovative ideas will differentiate them from their competitors. You cannot always come up with innovative ideas by yourself: sometimes through the collective engagement and dialogue of a team focusing on solving a particular problem, you come up with something that is the 1 + 1 = 3 scenario.

Everyone may be brilliant in their own right, but when you back it together, there's a catalyst and there's almost a quantum leap, which wouldn't have happened if people hadn't been together at that particular moment in time. The smartest companies will ultimately survive. That's why diversity is so important.

For me, innovation is about how we are responding to market needs as they are evolving. Do we understand the pace of change? Do we understand our clients' needs? Are we seeing opportunities to evolve our offerings to produce new things, different things, very quickly?

You don't always need A-list people or people who pass with As. People have traditionally argued that it's important to have the brightest people if you want to produce new ideas. I believe you need that to have diversity of thoughts and solutions; you need a diversity of people.

Today what's important is the generation of ideas and new knowledge. New services, products, philosophies and approaches to the world come from harnessing that collective energy of people – everyone within the organisation – and firing up people to produce new approaches to life.

We are sometimes restricted by our self-imposed limitations; we're also restricted by the paradigms determined by society and workplaces. Our biggest fear as female senior executives and leaders is the fear of failure. Because of fear, people don't step up.

It's very important to recognise fear and how to best manage it. Personally, I have many fears and anxieties. I've suddenly become afraid of stepping onto long, steep escalators, and I cannot explain why. I still cannot ride a bicycle properly nor jump across two stepping stones, even if they're only half a metre apart.

People see me as a highly competent, confident person. But despite all the speeches I've made in my life, I still get the heebie-jeebies whenever I have to speak in public. I am nervous for the first five minutes and always find myself saying a little prayer: "Let me do a good job of this." Affirmations like "I can do this" help as well.

There are times when I'm filled with nagging doubts. I tell myself: "I am going to mess up. Someone is going to find out that I don't know something. I didn't prepare well enough. I feel inadequate. I don't feel that I should step up onto the podium today." We've all heard these little voices of self-doubt in our heads at some time or the other. There are times when I've gone into a board meeting and I haven't been confident that I will be able to influence or shape a decision.

We need to be realistic: there are times when there will be gaps. No-one is perfect. You don't need to take yourself down for this. Women, in particular, are guilty of this. We're so aware of the negative voices or the criticism. We haven't always built up our self-esteem sufficiently well, so the smallest of things can take us down. We're often our own worst enemies because we judge ourselves so harshly, while the rest of the world thinks that what we've done is fantastic.

When these situations arise you need to find a way to centre yourself. You need to say: "I am going to give this my best shot. If they send me back to get more statistics or more spreadsheets or more data or to do more research, that's fine. I'm happy to come back a second time."

There are so many women who don't feel they are good enough. It boils down to a lack of self-belief, a lack of self-esteem and a lack of self-confidence. Self-belief is a big driver. Even when everything around you seems to be collapsing, you have to believe that you have what it takes and listen to the feedback trusted advisers are giving.

People tend to focus far too much on past failures. But you can't get everything right. You can't always have all the answers. Thomas Edison didn't always get it right. He tried many things before he got light bulbs to work. But he always learnt from his failures, and we should do the same. Sometimes, having failed, you ignite a spark that generates a whole new trajectory of thinking and a way of being.

Many of us get stuck in our own world view of not being good enough or of being inadequate, and we don't have the strength to be able to pull through the complexities of life. Self-belief is a deeply internal and personal thing, and personal mastery requires continuous work .

We speak very glibly about learning organisations, but do organisations actually tolerate mistakes? So-called learning organisations often say they allow people to learn through mistakes, but in reality, they have a very limited appetite for this. When people make mistakes, organisations lose money. There are times when forward-looking organisations may see money lost as an investment in learning.

Everyone is born with potential, but we're not all going to be CEOs. We all have the potential to become something great in and of ourselves. But there has to be balance: life is about so much more than checking boxes. It's about reflection, re-energising and re-fuelling yourself so you can operate optimally in all areas of your life. It's also about seeing the value of being present and being more effective human beings.

The joy of life is possible at any point of your life-cycle, but you might miss it in the blinding mist of 'busy-ness'. Identify what is holding you back if you feel that you are being held back, and then do something about it.

And have fun and let your hair down from time to time – it's good for you. Leading a balanced life – actually having a life – will also help you to perform far better in the workplace.

I do a lot of coaching and mentoring in my new role. Coaching and mentoring isn't easy. It's very difficult for people you are mentoring to make the changes, to overcome the setbacks and challenges they face. But it is most fulfilling to see people make those first steps towards unleashing their potential.

We have a well-defined body of knowledge around the importance and significance of mentorship – it's an accredited practice. We can see the tangible difference that it makes in people's lives.

Although I advise women to actively seek out mentors, I never consciously looked for a mentor myself, partly because I never knew that I needed to do this, and partly because mentors came to me in many different guises. Informal mentors include my parents, my teachers, Kevin, my professors at Harvard, Aletha Ling, Pravin Gordhan and Tom Boardman.

Many of the people I've stumbled across in the course of work or life in general, have taught me valuable lessons. I listened to these messages; I took them seriously and reflected on them.

Some of the people I've mentored have told me that they're being picked on or bullied at work. They feel they have no choice but to leave their current workplace. I always caution that this person will pop up elsewhere, or in another guise. We need to find ways to deal with people like this, so that we are not intimidated, subdued and overwhelmed by mischief-making tyrants who are generally self-serving, and have forgotten about the principles of *ubuntu* and servant leadership.

Bullying in the workplace is a problem in every industry, and it's easy to spot a bully. This is someone who belittles others, especially in front of other people. A bully is negative and criticises anything and everything. The bully's body language is aggressive; her/his tone of voice and facial expression support this. Bullies have a general lack of respect for others, especially their victims.

In our workplaces it has reached a new level of sophistication that makes it difficult to name. Although some bullying is reported and dealt with in terms of workplace policies and legislation, most of it happens under the radar. Bullies seek to inflict shame and humility on victims and this is often facilitated in hierarchical organisations where relationships are top-down, antagonistic, and not driven by respect. Power and disempowerment are at the very core of bullying behaviour.

At some stage in your career you will meet people who will tell you that what you do is insufficient, inadequate or unacceptable. You will find yourself walking out of the room with your tail between your legs. The reality is that you will need to walk into the same room again, so it's important to figure out what to do.

I always recommend having a conversation with this person afterwards. Listen to their feedback, and try to do something positive with it. Confronting the bully helps to understand intent, and understanding intent helps you to deal with the underlying issues and to take them on.

Kevin once told me how his best friend at primary school, Nigel Forbes, urged him to get even with the bully who beat him up every day for fun. On the day that he decided to return a punch, the bully really retaliated and beat him up good and solid. However, that was the last time – it never happened again.

The point is that you have to confront the bullying before it will end. I will never advocate violence as a means to resolving a problem, obviously, but I do want to emphasise the importance of confronting the problem head-on in order to deal with it decisively.

People feel vulnerable and overwhelmed in a bullying environment. They are subject to enormous stress and anxiety daily and are worn down by the continuing attacks. It affects adults just as it affects children, and has devastating and deep-seated effects on our psyches.

Bullying must be dealt with as it impacts on self-esteem and self-confidence; it also silences people into submission. You have a choice to either stand up for yourself, or to walk away. You cannot excel when you are constantly thinking that someone is out to get you. You need to be able to rise above this.

By examining our own vulnerabilities and triggers, we will be able to respond to these situations, so whenever you feel fearful, anxious, hurt, nervous, or less confident, understand the source of your fears and work on how you might overcome this. You need to be in tune with yourself and recognise your feelings as you work through a stimulus-response emotion.

While there are people who care and might be able to assist you, it starts with being true to yourself. We are all human, and fears ebb and flow depending on the complexities we are facing.

Chapter 16

South Africa today

The death of Nelson Mandela, our former president, on 5 December 2013, affected me very deeply. We all knew for a long time that Madiba was very ill, but his passing, nevertheless, proved an emotional roller-coaster for me, for many South Africans, and the world.

I returned home from dinner with friends that night, and I turned on the television. A few minutes before midnight, the news broadcast was interrupted for a special announcement from President Jacob Zuma: our beloved Madiba had passed away at 8.50pm.

I went to bed reflecting on what Madiba's death meant for our country and for the African continent as a whole. Madiba was well-respected as a leader both in South Africa and globally. If we only did ten percent of what Madiba did, we could move this country forward significantly.

On hearing of his passing I felt shock and despair and the emotional rush that comes from the death of someone of such stature in the world. I also found myself asking the big question: "What is the journey forward going to be?" What I saw the following day was a South Africa united in a way that I hadn't seen for a very long time. In the weeks leading up to the elections in 2014, I had felt an overwhelming sense that our country and our nation were deeply fragmented.

One of the first emails I received about his death was from my Professor of Education at Harvard, Eleanor Duckworth. The email read: "I am very sorry for your loss today. An enormous loss for all of us."

I replied: "Heard the news around midnight last night. I gulped away my tears and developed a new resolve to take the vision forward personally in whatever way I can."

I also received an email from Bombardier Airspace in Canada, to which I replied: "Thank you so much. We all feel that he has been part of our lives, even if we did not know him first hand. It is as though we know him. The true father of our nation, his leadership in breaking the shackles of apartheid, his courage to transform society, his unyielding effort to liberate people is so profound. We salute his life and his dedication to freedom, equality."

Madiba inspired and unified people, and we can all learn from his compassion. One of the things that moved me deeply was his view on education: "… the most powerful weapon we have to change the world." I will continue to hold onto that vision for as long as I live. I will strive to make every day a Mandela Day.

All over the world people have really got behind what an amazing man Madiba was, but I'm not sure that all South Africans have properly understood this. If we're serious about Madiba's legacy, we need to think very earnestly about how we are going to keep it alive. The only way we can actually make his spirit live on is for us to emulate the way he lived and the difference he made.

If every South African could only take on some portion of what they think they can actually do to make that flame burn on beyond the here and now, and get beyond the emotional response we initially had, we have a great opportunity to take this country up a few notches in terms of dealing with our current challenges, be they economic, social or political. We have an opportunity to unify the nation around the purpose that Madiba put out there for us.

I had lunch with my friends Italia Boninelli and Sandy Mohonathan in Sandton the weekend after Madiba's passing. I saw thousands of flowers in Mandela Square and people – old and young, local and foreign – paying their respects. And I felt a strong sense of loss and celebration at the same time. But while I felt a terrible sense of loss, I also felt the need to celebrate this remarkable man's life. Madiba was larger than life. While he may have left us physically, all the seeds that he planted need to be harvested by us. We need to keep nurturing Madiba's vision.

For me Madiba went beyond being some sort of Father Africa. Madiba was also a son of Africa. He remains a global icon. We loved Madiba as the father of our nation, the architect of democracy. Very few of us will ever see such a person again. Having experienced Madiba's leadership, we cannot slip back into anything less.

Madiba could have waged war against the people who hated him. This would've taken the country back decades, but he was big enough, compassionate enough and knew this was not the way to go. We can learn from this. There was no revenge, no hatred. He promoted respect for everyone, irrespective of where they came from. He also promoted justice, equality and humanity.

We've lost our humanity in many respects. We've eroded it and continue to erode it as we squabble over the crumbs that fall onto the table, instead of trying to build the pie and make it bigger for everyone. We need to keep Madiba's dream alive. We need to reconcile our differences. We don't always need to agree. We can live in the ethos of reconciliation. This is a very powerful concept, one he introduced, and one we must never forget.

Madiba left a great void in the leadership of our country. Today, South Africans are looking for a new kind of leadership.

I'm often asked what I think of the quality of leadership in general in South Africa today.

I'm worried about how the way in which the moral fabric in South Africa is being eroded; and I worry about youth unemployment, poverty and continued inequities. We're sitting on a ticking time bomb from a youth development perspective. Young people are becoming impatient. People are growing tired of empty promises.

We need to get serious about growing our economy, and about pulling unemployed people into the economy. We can talk as much as we like about youth development and jobs, but unless we get the economy to grow, we are not going to create jobs.

It's possible to have different sectors of the economy that are labour intensive. We could, for example, put people who have never had a job before into entry-level jobs, help them to restore their pride and dignity. Only then can we can deal with the socio-economic issues that we face.

We have the Sectoral Education and Training Authorities (SETAs), and hundreds of millions of rands are poured into skills development, but this is not being channelled out effectively to build the skills and talent pipeline that the country so desperately needs. Some scarce and critical skills vacancies haven't been filled in years. There is a lot of talk, but very little is actually happening to turn this around.

Education is fundamental to changing the world. Government spends approximately R200-billion on education, and there are twenty-seven thousand schools struggling to find and keep good teachers. They are also struggling to ensure that the infrastructure is maintained, and that our children get a decent standard of education. I am worried about children being able to read, write and do mathematics.

At the same time, there are many children who are not in schools, but wandering around our streets begging, heading up households of their siblings. Many are victims of rape and violence. Our society has been unable to respond effectively to this.

We now have the National Development Plan (NDP), which is the 2030 strategic plan for South Africa. We have spent more time critiquing it rather than being the active citizens it calls us to be, and to make a difference where we can, instead of waiting for others to do it for us.

I believe South Africans are looking for a new kind of leadership. They're tired of seeing the pillaging and plundering and the accumulation of personal wealth, versus making a difference in the world. The latter is the sort of leadership that we need to build a great South Africa.

I am proudly South African. If you asked me what the one thing is that South Africa needs right now, I'd say it is a unity of vision for this country and a strong sense of common purpose, as South Africans, to build cohesion in our country. If only this could be the single-minded focus of every leader in South Africa we would be able to collectively focus on economic growth and social development.

There have been times during the past twenty years when no matter who you were, you were so proud to be part of this awesome country. The things reported on in our press were also very different. Today, we vacillate between that and low troughs of despair. This is part of our maturation process as we grow – it's not all going to be perfect. We have, unfortunately, not yet been able to define a shared vision that will unify us and propel us forward.

The preamble to our Constitution is a huge anchor and inspiration for me, so I read it out loud at almost every presentation I make, hoping that it will inspire others to heal the wounds of the past, and build a better world for all. This is what Madiba's life was all about, and we need to make sure that we continue to do that. We need to do some hard work to get South Africa back on track. This requires us to be extraordinary and courageous. If Mandela could broker a deal with the apartheid government, how much more is possible?

It never occurred to me, initially, to view Madiba lying in state. I put it off as I saw the difficulty of getting to Pretoria and the logistical challenges associated with getting into the Union Buildings. After some reflection, however, I realised that this was something I needed to do so, I asked Kevin to drop me off as close to the Union Buildings as possible.

I stood in the queue and reflected on Madiba's life.

It was a huge honour to see him. I was deeply moved and felt very privileged to see him lying in state, the father of our nation, who achieved so much. I could feel a deep sense of connection. I drew a sense of purpose out of seeing him there. I felt that I needed to try to continue to move his legacy forward to build a country that is substantially connected to pillars of democracy, equality and freedom in the way in which he interpreted this.

Given what has happened in my own life, I've always found Madiba's love for children very moving. However each year, throughout the sixteen days of activism around violence against women and children, I continue to see violations. Many wounds and much pain continue to exist, and the matter of abuse, violence and brutality against women continues to occupy our daily TV and newspapers.

We can't sweep this matter under the carpet any longer or allow it to be lost in the lists of things to be done in a democracy. Madiba said that a society needs to reflect on itself seriously if it starts to prey on its own children. This is critical.

We need the kind of leadership that's going to be respected by the rest of the world. When the dust settles, will we forget, or will we have stepped up our game and created a more just society?

Terrible things happened under apartheid that have affected people and their families personally. Families were torn apart. I only have to think of Kevin's family: the Zinn family are third or fourth generation German. They came to South Africa from Namibia.

As part of social engineering, in the early 1950s Kevin's father, together with his siblings, had to choose whether the family wanted to be classified white or coloured. One of Kevin's aunts chose to be classified white and married a white man. Kevin's father chose to be classified as coloured as most of his friends were already classified as coloured. Besides, Reuben had a serious interest in dating a coloured woman – Kevin's mother! Had Reuben not been coloured, he would have been unable to marry her. That was the tyranny of the Mixed Marriage and Group Areas Act: it split families apart forever.

Kevin and his siblings, Allan and Sandy, have never met some of the Zinn family. I once asked Kevin's dad whether he'd like to see his sister. "I want nothing to do with her because she decided to align herself with the apartheid regime," he replied.

Twenty years into our democracy you'd expect people to have shifted their thinking. Many haven't. Deep-rooted assumptions and prejudices cause people to ask inappropriate questions and to behave in a racist and hurtful manner.

It's a rude awakening to realise that there are people in South Africa who believe we should stop talking about diversity and transformation. Uninformed and ignorant, and not always *au fait* with the true facts, they typically say: "It's about time we moved on."

We can't move on as if nothing ever happened because people are still in pain. There are many South Africans who are still very angry about a lot of things that happened to them, and who can blame them? People are still hurting from the ills of apartheid and discrimination, many of which continue in a new guise in our democracy.

We cannot pretend that this doesn't exist. We have to act and ensure that in everything we do, every day, we take this into account. It starts with our own behaviour. Men and women, as active citizens, need to build a society based on social and environmental justice. This is the foundation of a non-sexist, non-racial society in South Africa.

As much as we would like to create the kind of South Africa that Oliver Tambo referred to as "a country where there will be neither whites nor blacks, just South Africans, free and united in diversity," we need to deal with and heal the divisions of the past. Whether we like it or not, some of us are still more equal than others. This needs to change.

I come from a place where social injustice was very prevalent in our lives as a family and as a community. Social injustice is still something that as South Africans, we have to work at and think about really hard. We need to ensure that we're giving everyone an opportunity to contribute to building our economy, and the opportunity to benefit from participating in the economy. None of us is fully free when others around us live in poverty. The world is watching our decisions and our choices.

From a social justice point of view, there are still many elements where the sophistication around understanding social injustice is very limited. People don't have a sense of just how bad the social injustices still are, and how deeply-seated they are in our society.

Accountability needs to be infused into both the public and private sectors, because unless we start behaving as responsible citizens we're going to face some deep-seated problems. The challenge is that it creating a just and equitable South Africa starts with me and it starts with you.

CHAPTER 17

MY LIFE'S JOURNEY

I've spoken about my life's journey at various forums, from business schools to organisations, at events celebrating Women's Day, to church groups and school children. And there's always a horrifying moment before you're about to make a speech, when people read your biography. People will say: "Shirley is a professor with a doctorate from Harvard, and she's held several senior positions in large corporates in South Africa and globally. Wow, you've had it all. What a lovely story. You must've been so privileged. You're so lucky."

Some people are able to identify with my story when I tell them about growing up in poverty on the Cape Flats. But when I get to the really personal stuff, where I was broke doing my doctorate at Harvard, or when Kevin and I lost our only child, or the times where I've hit an emotional rock bottom, everyone just sits there, astonished. You can literally see their jaws drop. And it's at that point that we all realise that it's our humanity that we have in common.

When we strip away the trappings of title, status, rank or power, there's a unity about who we are: we're all human. We all have our complexities and the challenges that life will continue to throw at us.

Vulnerability isn't a weakness. It's about being and becoming a better version of who we are in this world. We're constantly in the process of becoming, and we never really quite arrive. The becoming is about moving towards full self-actualisation and fulfilment within ourselves and with the external environment, and it's about how we deal with forces and social engineering that seek to impose limitations and barriers to our growth, success and making a difference.

It's like the metaphor of ascending the mountain, summiting, standing at the top for a few seconds, and seeing the range of other summits that you still have to get to. Sometimes when I'm running half marathons, a voice in my head says: "I don't know why I'm doing this. I could be sitting somewhere, with my feet up, relaxing … but I have to keep going."

When I'm running up a steep slope that doesn't seem to want to end, and I'm out of energy and I'm tired and I just want to sit down on the pavement and catch my breath, I think to myself: "Does the road wind uphill all the way? The answer is always: "Yes, to the very end." (*Up-Hill*, By Christina Rossetti).

The road is going to be a winding one, and there are going to be many summits that I still have to reach in my lifetime. I thought the doctorate was going to be the hardest thing I'd ever do in my life, but it was just a building block for the next thing in life, for the next level of complexity to come.

Choosing a title for my autobiography was the easy part. Swimming upstream has been a constant throughout my entire life. Struggle has been key to my endeavours. Grit has pulled me through.

Swimming upstream is an act of risk that can potentially have devastating outcomes. It's part of my decision to live a life without regrets, and to its absolute fullest. Salmon swim upstream to spawn. Many die on the way there, or on the way back. We have to work hard and be that committed to the challenging course of life. We need to view every step as an opportunity to learn and to prepare for the next step.

Impossible is possible. It's possible to move forward irrespective of what hardships and setbacks present themselves, as they inevitably will. Swimming upstream is a metaphor for pushing my internal boundaries. It's the inner dialogue that I have with myself about what I can and can't do.

I'm very cognisant of the fact that I'm not invincible and I can't do it alone, but together we can – *potest qui vult* – he/she/it who wills, is able.

Even today, I still don't believe I've arrived; I'm still in the process of being and becoming. I'm still swimming up the stream, perhaps not as hard as before, but I'm on a journey of self-actualisation to try and be the very best I can be at all times, and perhaps tomorrow I might be a better version of what I am today. So now, when a challenge presents itself, I ask myself: "Is this a ridiculous thought, or is it something that I can actually achieve?"

I've always felt that I've been working against all the odds. At every turn, every day I've felt that I've been working to get through boundaries and barriers. I've constantly pushed myself through all of this, while listening to voices on the way, taking things on board, being inspired and also dealing with inevitable setbacks, but picking myself up time and time again.

I share my story to demonstrate that it can be done. I'm the first to acknowledge that I'm not always upbeat. There are times when I too struggle, especially on the days leading up to the anniversary of Jamie's death. I know this is happening, so I do something about it to get through these difficult times. It mostly involves spending time with people I love.

I want to encourage young women to push themselves harder and to be the very best that they can be. Remember Nelson Mandela's words: "It seems impossible, until it's done." I caution, however, that there will be setbacks. We know that all salmon don't always make it upstream, but we should never, ever give up.

It's important to acknowledge that swimming upstream isn't for everyone, and it's a conscious decision. We shouldn't judge people if they decide that they don't want to study further, or if they're not interested in climbing the career ladder, or pushing hard to get to the top. Some people move diagonally. Some people just love the space that they're in and want to hold that space. We need to respect this decision.

When people make these choices it's important to understand the consequences of their decision. You can't turn the clock back, but you can continue to progress. Time is not the only barrier to success. Especially in South Africa, we have had 20 years of freedom since 1994, and while many women have broken through the glass ceiling, in general women continue to be challenged socially, economically and politically.

There are many contrasts in our society between the haves and the have-nots, rich and poor, employed and unemployed, and negativity and optimism. We have come a long way on our journey to democracy and a non-racist, non-sexist society. But we still have a long way to go.

I'm very cognisant of the fact that many women see me as a role model. Many have said this to me and it's very humbling. It's a great honour and not something that I take lightly. As Dickens might have written, I've really experienced the "best of times and the worst of times". In my own life, I've seen the pendulum swing between extremes of joy and pain, and everything else is in the middle. Sometimes one takes one step forward and two steps back in a single day – it happens to all of us.

Doing well, or achieving success, means different things to different people. Does success mean you have reached the pinnacle of your career? Does "well" mean that you have been appointed president? Does it mean you have lots of money in the bank?

If you asked Mother Teresa or Gandhi or Mandela, or people we believe are icons, it's usually about the difference that they've made to the world. It's not about them. When you've reached that level, it's about selflessness and the impact your life has on those around you.

And the higher you move towards this sort of service to humanity, the more accountability and responsibility you have for what goes on in the world, in your societies and in your communities. We all have a responsibility to give back.

I hope to be able to say that I've managed to shift the needle on poverty, around the future of children and women in our country, and around the future of education. Having been privileged enough to have obtained a very good education, I hope to have planted some seeds about the importance of education, and more specifically, the importance of quality education.

When my life draws to a close, I'd like to be able to say that I've made a small contribution using everything that I had at my disposal, be it through my work, or through my personal journey. And remember as you make this journey, that every day is a new beginning. I will continue to swim upstream as I journey through the future chapters of life.

I am very grateful for everything life has been to date. I am grateful to those around me who supported and inspired me throughout this journey. As Melody Beattie writes, "Gratitude unlocks the fullness of life. It turns what we have into enough, and more. It turns denial into acceptance, chaos to order, confusion to clarity. It can turn a meal into a feast, a house into a home, a stranger into a friend."

My challenge to women is to be the best you can be, in the space that you choose to be in. Don't let anyone tell you that you can't. I'm reminded of what Martin Luther King Jr. said: "Everybody can be great ... because anybody can serve. You don't have to have a college degree to serve. You don't have to make your subject and verb agree to serve. You only need a heart full of grace. A soul generated by love."

THE END

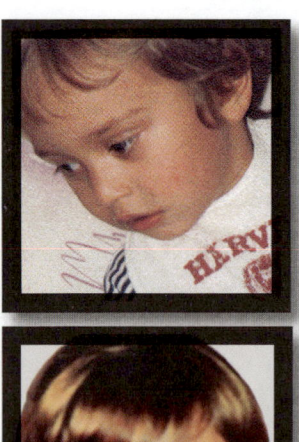

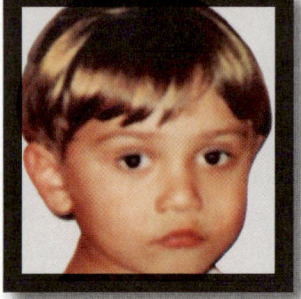

Jamie

Jamie – the Harvard baby

Shirley and Jamie – first day of school

Shirley in Sub A
Square Hill Primary

Kevin and Shirley
getting married

Shirley Zinn with her
sister Merle Anthony

Shirley and Kevin

Memories

Jamie Zinn and his cousin, Erin Anthony

Shirley and her mom 1st Birthday

Ma Wyngaard

Shirley and her parents at the age of one

Shirley and Kevin
Doctoral Graduation Harvard 1997

*Finishing Two Oceans
half marathon*

FAMILY MEMORIES OF JAMIE

Erin, my beautiful niece, my sister Merle's only child, who so sadly passed away on 2 April 2015 at the tender age of seventeen, wrote this piece in honour of her cousin Jamie in 2014:

I always used to hear stories about how shy and quiet Jamie was when it came to socialising with people. I also heard how good he was at sports, especially swimming. So when he passed away, I thought what better way to honour him than by swimming in his honour and trying to achieve all the great things I believed he would have achieved if he was still with us today. I was seven years old when I joined the school's swimming team and now I am swimming for a club. I have represented Western Province in swimming. I have been swimming for ten years now and it's grown into my greatest passion and love. I owe it all to Jamie. He is the reason I love the sport so much and why I will never give up, because I know every time I swim, I swim for him.

This is what Allan (Kevin's brother) wrote as he reflected on Jamie's passing:

The untimely death of my nephew Jamie probably taught me the biggest management lesson of my career – something I will get back to later.

Some broader family members thought that Jamie was a strange child, an introvert who did not warm up quickly to others in company, but preferred to remain close to his loving and doting mom and dad. However, I found him warm and curious.

Perhaps the circumstances in which I interacted with Jamie when they lived in Elardus Park, Pretoria, when I had cause to stay overnight whilst on work business in Gauteng, assisted in this assessment. After arriving at their residence (shared with Grandpa Reuben and Grandma Jean) I was easily coaxed to have a dip in the pool with Jamie, who thrived in that environment. In the evenings after his bath, I was invited by Jamie to read to him or to view a DVD – always a specific one about volcanoes. I remember when he was this age, he had particular favourites, and inevitably one knew what was going to be suggested by Jamie. I found this interesting as an educationalist, that he preferred really getting to know something in depth rather than flitting around with variety.

To return to the life's lesson alluded to earlier. I was with my immediate family on our first vacation to Australia when we heard the tragic news via our cousin Renee. After ascertaining that Kevin and Shirley survived even though Shirley had been seriously injured, I recall wondering what one says to a brother who has lost a child (his only child) and remember just wanting to return as quickly as possible to just be with family in SA – even though I felt so powerless to be of any real help.

That experience has really affected how I have responded to crisis situations going forward. When colleagues say 'We have a crisis,' I reply 'Has anyone died?' It may sound facetious, but I recall Jamie, and know that any challenge that is not death itself, is one we can still hope to be resolved.

So, I will forever feel deeply connected to Jamie – both in life and death.

This is what Granny Jean and Grandpa Reuben had to say:

I often think of Jamie. I mysteriously receive feathers that appear from nowhere from time to time, and it comforts me to know that he is around. He loved birds, especially weavers, when he was alive. He loved the outdoors and the wind in his hair.

When I saw him at the airport for the first time, when he arrived from America, I knew he was a special child, "our angel", on loan to us for a short time.

I used to love pushing Jamie in his pram – small pram with big baby in it. We went out even on Lansdowne Road when Kevin warned me never to do this as it was too dangerous – too many dogs and traffic. Jamie loved every moment of this, hair blowing in the wind, a real happy-chappy. Even at Sun City, we walked the entire place flat together. He loved the shuttle as travelling in buses was a novelty.

He loved his little plastic black push-bike, gave Jeannie a few heart-attacks with all his bravery on this bike at the time. I couldn't buy him ice-creams, it was too expensive. His parents were very fussy about what he ate and as his grandmother I felt bad that he did not know what an ice-cream was at the age of three. Uncle Georgie had to tell him what to do with his first ice cream.

He loved his dogs Tyson, Watson and Jacky. Jeannie's sisters used to quiver with stress when Jamie played with the big German Shepherds in the dog's kennel and she couldn't find him. 3pm was play-time with the dogs.

His happy days were the best at the Sun City Valley of the Waves – he used to cling to me when the hooter went off for the waves to come, he went crazy when the waves rolled in. He loved swimming in the sea and jumping into rivers with his father.

He had a great appetite and ate heartily. He loved mince curry and sushi. He used to stand on the chair to look into the pot as Pops cooked dinner. He received a gold star certificate at school for cake decoration.

Jamie went everywhere with Jeannie. One day I went to the post office to post a birthday card for Uncle Bowie in May. I forgot the card and went back home to pick up the card, and slipped down the wet pathway to the house. Jamie was sitting in the car waiting for me to come back, Pops was watching TV, and I had slipped and broken my ankle. Eventually Jamie came to investigate, and when Jamie said that there was "no bleed", but went to call Pops to help me up. I had to be taken to the hospital and put it into a cast.

Jamie was an orderly child. His routine in the afternoon after school was homework, swimming, computer, cooking dinner with Pops. He even had his own apron.

He loved his kick-boxing classes – at the age of four, he went to gym – the youngest in his class. He received a yellow belt, as well as a few others as he was graded and made progress as the youngest in the class. I had to sit there, put my gym bag where he could see "Jeannie's gym bag" and know that she was still there. He loved his running at school and received a few prizes for this.

We used to go the shopping malls together and he would go into the shop like a "big boy". The moment he could not see Jeannie, he would anxiously start to call for her in the shop.

I think about when he was three years old how he loved his walks in Elardus Park in Pretoria and chased me around the mulberry bush down the road, which he loved.

He loved to swim after school every afternoon winter summer or fall. We played touch-touch – I was the big fish! He laughed like crazy. I still have not been able to swim in the pool because my memories of Jamie and our enjoyment still make me sad.

He was six years old when he taught me to work on the computer. He had learnt how to work the computer from watching his mother. I was completely computer illiterate at the time. He introduced me to it and I could write a letter, save it. He was a great teacher.

The last day at school, just before the December 2002 holidays, I went with Jamie to the school year-end church service. Each learner received a little card with a Bible verse on it. I still have his one that read: John 3:16 "For God so loved the world that he gave his only begotten son so that everyone who believes in him may not die."

I remember our flight to Cape Town in December 2002. Jamie decided that he would look after Pops and me on the plane. I think he must have known he was not going to be coming back from this Cape Town trip. He had a sixth sense – thinking back, I felt this. He was quiet and reflective on the plane. He didn't even eat anything, which was unusual.

The day he passed on, some part of me also left me. Those seven years with Jamie were the happiest years of our lives. He brought life, laughter and joy to us all. We are grateful for the seven years of Jamie.

Memories of Jamie from Ma and Pa Jeftha and my sister, Merle Anthony:

Pa:

The birth of our two daughters, (Shirley and Merle) was a glorious gift from God. Also two grand-children, Jamie and Erin. Jamie's short life on this earth has given me beautiful memories.

For example, Jamie coming for his holiday at Christmas time. He says, "Pa let's run from the gate to the garage." One day he said, "Pa, how come you can run so fast?" I said, when you are grown up, you will also be able to run fast.

There are many other memories, the guava tree in the back yard and Baby Land, the crèche. We used to sing to him when it was time to sleep. He loved "What a mighty God we serve". I loved that song and sang it at Harvard University at Shirley's graduation.

Ma:

Jamie, a beautiful gift, a blessing of a grandson. He was a lovely chubby baby boy. We had so much fun with him. He loved to sing with us "Mine, mine, mine, Jesus is mine" and "What a mighty God we serve".

He loved playing with the dogs, and they loved him too. He liked to hide the dogs in the washing basket.

One day we went to the beach in Simon's Town. It was very windy there and we decided to leave. Jamie was very upset about this change of plan. We said we would take him to see the penguins. But, he was not happy. We decided to go home. He said, "Pa, can't your car ride faster?"

He loved to play cricket with Pa.

When he lived in Pretoria, he came for Christmas holidays to Ma and Pa's house in Cape Town. In November, he packed his toys, because he was coming to Cape Town.

On 3 January 2003, we received the bad news of the accident on the N2. Jamie died that day. We were very saddened by his death. We will always love him and carry him in our hearts.

Aunty Merle:

Shirley and Kevin came for my wedding in December 1994 and told us that Shirley was expecting a baby. We were all thrilled at having a baby in the family. Jamie was born 24 May 1995 in Boston, USA, and they all came back to Cape Town in July that year. Jamie was such a beautiful boy. Everything we dreamed of having. Shirley went back to work in November 1995 and Ma and Pa Jeftha took care of Jamie. He was the centre of their lives.

FROM: Renate Graeler (Jamie's godmother in Germany)

I saw Jamie first when he was just a couple of weeks old. He was such a cute, lovely and friendly baby.

I really felt honoured when Kevin and Shirley asked me to be one of his godmothers.

Unfortunately we lived in different countries so I didn't get the chance to see him very often. I remember that he loved to run barefoot. He was much faster than with shoes on. He proved that in one of the sports events in his school where I was able to watch him.

I remember that he loved sushi – I've never seen any kid enjoying sushi like he did. To be honest, I've never seen anyone enjoying sushi like he did. He really loved the stuff.

Ice cream, on the other side, is a completely different story. I was with him and his grandparents when he had his first taste of ice cream. He was just a baby then and his face said it all – what disgusting stuff! It was so funny to watch his face.

He was a very active kid, playing outside with the dogs, always doing something. I can remember that he was chasing the chickens in my mum's field when he was a toddler.

He was raised in a happy family and that showed – he was a happy kid, always smiling. And he had a really charming smile. South Africa in a very unstable and dangerous country but he still had a really good childhood. He felt safe.

It's a shame that he didn't get the chance to grow into this tall, handsome and wonderful young man that he would have been.

But it is this happy, smiling little boy who will always stay in my heart.

Dr Sandy Zinn, Kevin's sister and Jamie's godmother:

Every time I look at the miniature koala bear toy clinging to my door handle, I think of Jamie. It was the last gift he gave me, a memento of his recent trip to Australia. My heart does a tiny flip each time I watch the series Extant on television because the humanoid boy is the image of Jamie.

Jamie was Jean and Reuben's booitjie. Jamie could attack a mango Jeanie-style – messy, mushy, and mouth-watering. Nothing delicate or dainty. At 5pm every day he had his "sundowner" with Rubes.

I remember Jamie as a self-contained lad: loved his dogs, loved the outdoors, and with an imagination of note. Visiting Jamie in his bedroom was a labyrinth of invisible wires you had to climb over or duck under at his instructions before you could reach him on the far end of the room. Then you had to hear about volcanoes in detail before watching a volcano movie with him for the nth time.

Now here's a secret: Jamie had some of his aunty's traits. He liked order. The cutlery drawer was his domain. Perfectly compartmentalised cutlery silos. Attaboy! He disliked wearing shoes. When I was a child, I seldom wore shoes unless required for formal occasions. The problem, I suspect, was we were both pigeon-toed. Shoes just cramped our style.

I wish we could have spent more time together. There was so much I wanted to find out about Jamie who was born a day before my birthday. It was not to be. Jamie's untimely death has left an open wound that somehow refuses to heal completely.

About the Author

SHIRLEY ZINN

Prof Shirley Zinn is the former Human Resources Director of Standard Bank South Africa and Deputy Global Head of Human Resources for the Standard Bank Group. She has since registered her own company: Shirley Zinn Consulting, which provides consulting and advisory services in HR, Transformation, Leadership and Education.

Prior to this she was the Group Executive HR at Nedbank. Before this, she was the General Manager for Human Resources at the South African Revenue Service (SARS). She is also an Extraordinary Professor at the University of Pretoria's Department of Human Resource Management and is the Past President of the Institute for People Management South Africa.

She started her career as a secondary school teacher of English, then moved to the University of the Western Cape where she lectured in Teacher Education. After this, she served at Southern Life as Training Manager and then moved to the Department of Public Service and Administration's: South African Management Development Institute, in Pretoria as Director. She held the position of Executive Employment Equity at Computer Configurations Holdings. Before her appointment at SARS, she filled the role of Regional Human Resources Director for Middle East and Africa for Reckitt Benckiser, a global company listed on the London Stock Exchange.

She is currently the Chairman of DHL: Global Forwarding SA, and a Non-Executive Director on the Boards of AdvTech, Tuesday Consulting, Business Engage, Sygnia Asset Management, and the Boston Consulting Group SA. She is a Trustee on the DHL Foundation, the Nedbank Eyethu Community Trust, the Orbis Africa Charity, and the Chairman of Starfish Greathearts Foundation. She also serves on the Advisory Boards of Monash, African Society for Talent Development, and the University of Pretoria's Faculty of Economic and Management Sciences. She is the President for the Harvard Alumni Association South Africa and a Fellow of the Institute of Directors SA. Shirley also previously served as the Chair of the Institute of Bankers, and on the Council of TUT.

She is a mentor to several women across multiple industries, particularly financial services.

She has presented at national and international conferences as a keynote speaker.

She holds a BA (University of the Western Cape); Higher Diploma in Education (University of the Western Cape); B.Ed Honours (UNISA); M.Ed (University of the Western Cape); Ed.M (Harvard) and Doctorate in Education (Ed.D) (Harvard).

She was awarded the Top Woman in Business and Government and Top Executive in Corporate South Africa.by Topco Media in 2008. She also was recognized by the Black Business Quarterly and received the Award for Top Woman in Business and Government and most Visionary Woman in 2008. She also received an award from the World Human resources Congress in Mumbai in 2007 and 2013 respectively for Excellence in Global HR Leadership. In 2012, was listed in the Top 30 Wonder Women in South Africa by the Wits Business Journal. She also completed her seventh Two Oceans Half Marathon in April 2015.

CONTACT DETAILS:
Email: szinn@iafrica.com
Cellphone: +27 82 9003143

Acknowledgements

I would like to express my sincere gratitude to the many people who saw me through this book; to all those who urged me to write my story when I did not think I had one, for those who provided unwavering support and talked things over, read, wrote, offered comments, challenged me, assisted in the editing and the proofreading, and those who inspired me. A huge thank you to you.

Writing this book has been daunting, cathartic and got me to reflect deeply on my life and career journey, and the events and people involved along the way.

Firstly, I want to thank my husband, Kevin Zinn, who supported and encouraged me throughout, and without whom this book would never have been written. Kevin, you have been my rock and inspiration.

I dedicate this book to our son, Jamie Zinn, our only child, whose tragic passing on at the age of seven in January 2003, gave me a renewed sense of purpose to make a difference in the world. Words cannot express how much we miss you.

A special tribute goes to my beautiful niece, Erin Anthony, the only child of my sister and brother-in-law, Merle and Mark Anthony, who was cousin and soul-mate to Jamie and who passed away due to a brain tumour at 17 years of age on the 2 April 2015 as I was writing this book. So much potential, so much zest for life, and so much promise – gone too soon.

My deep gratitude goes to my sister, Merle, my parents, James and Rosemarie Jeftha, my parents-in-law, Reuben and Jean Zinn, my maternal and paternal grandparents, and extended family, especially Aunty Joan Kearns, my godmother, for allowing me to follow my dreams throughout my childhood and for their ongoing unconditional love.

My sincere thanks also go to my incredible teachers, principals, lecturers, professors, colleagues, clients, institutions and organisations that I have worked with which have stretched me intellectually and professionally.

To my friends, of whom there are too many to mention, thank you for your love and believing in me, and most of all, for keeping me sane.

To Carol Butcher, thank you for helping me to put my first thoughts onto paper.

I would especially like to acknowledge and thank Wilhelm and Sharon Crous and Cia Joubert from KR for encouraging me to publish this book and advising me throughout the authoring of the book.

Mandy Collins, thank you for your professional editorial services, advice and energy. You are a true gem.

To Prof. Jonathan Jansen, thank you for being a great role model and an inspiration to many in South Africa and the world. Thank you for writing a compelling and incisive foreword to this book.

Each one of you has made an indelible impact on my life. My life has been enriched beyond measure because of you. For that, I am eternally grateful.

My humble hope is that, through telling my story, I will be able to inspire and touch the lives of many. If my story is able to change the life of just one person, then this book will have served its purpose.